POEMCITY
ANTHOLOGY
2025

PoemCity
KELLOGG-HUBBARD LIBRARY

· ANTHOLOGY **2025** ·

Montpelier, Vermont

PoemCity Anthology 2025 is the third book in an annual series of PoemCity anthologies. Release Date: April 1, 2025.

All Rights Reserved.
Printed in the USA.

Paperback ISBN: 978-1-57869-193-7

Published by Rootstock Publishing
an imprint of Ziggy Media LLC
Montpelier, VT 05602
info@rootstockpublishing.com
www.rootstockpublishing.com

Compiled by the Kellogg-Hubbard Library
135 Main Street, Montpelier, VT 05502
info@kellogghubbard.org
www.kellogghubbard.org

Designed by Dana Dwinell-Yardley (ddydesign.com).

Cover Art: Monica DiGiovanni, "Eclipse Ensō #2" ©2023, Ink and pigment on watercolor paper (www.monicadigiovanni.com).

Contents

Introduction i

PART ONE: POEMS

a darned shame's antithesis 3
Rick Agran, Worcester

Accretion 4
Alexander and Liam, Montpelier

Morning Dew on a Rose Petal 5
Amelie, age 9

Born 6
Ina Anderson, South Royalton

Looking Up in the
Windy Woods 7
Cara M.L. Arduengo, Barre

A mother, A daughter, A child 8
Asher, age 17

From Time to Time 9
S. Atwood, East Montpelier

Blue 10
Augie, age 7

Fiddleheads 11
Charles Barasch, Plainfield

Astral Projection 12
Ann Barrett, Marshfield

Musings From My Paddleboard 13
Kathy Barrows, Worcester

Settler 14
Julia Barstow, East Montpelier

Waves 15
J. E. Beatson, Jericho

Dare to Dream 16
Jacqueline Beecher, South Burlington

Ground's a-Bullin' 17
Kim Allen Bent, Montpelier

Listen 18
Neville Berle, Montpelier

To the Cabinet in the Ladies
Bathroom at the Doubletree
by Hilton Denver 19
Sarah Birgé, Montpelier

Climb 20
Julia Boles, Montpelier

Fellow Workers 21
Stephanie Boucher, East Montpelier

Marsh Seasons 22
Rebecca Bowen, Montpelier

Reaching 23
Anne Bower, South Pomfret

Five Miles from the Fire 24
Jo Bower, East Montpelier

The Smell of Fur 25
Scott Boyd, Stowe

Blue Tarp 26
Donna Bramley, South Burlington

Molde Beltza 27
Waters Breedlove, Montpelier

Anyhow 28
Jenn Brown, Montpelier

Wings 29
Mark Brown, Calais

Ireland by Train
(Dublin to Wexford) 30
Megan Buchanan, Putney

Untitled 31
Cheryl Burghdurf, Middlesex

Dusk 32
wayne f burke, Barre

January Morning 33
Ana Burtnett, Worcester

Yes, the Duct Tape You Use
Matters 34
Sue D. Burton, Burlington

a place inside a place 35
JT Butler, Duxbury

Chickadees 36
Barry Cahoon, Danville

Cardinal Love 37
Dave Cavanagh, Burlington

Precious Lives 38
Susan Chickering, East Montpelier

What is a Flower 39
Chloe, age 8

Desire Lines 40
Alice Christian, Colchester

At the Core 41
Peter L Clark, Woodbury

Storms Outside and Inside 42
Conor Isaiah Cleveland, Williamstown

Ode to Spring 43
Micki Colbeck, Strafford

In and Out of the Cold 44
PH Coleman, South Burlington

Apples on The Shelf
Martha's Kitchen 1969   45
Carol Johnson Collins, South Duxbury

the one about johnny spaniel   46
Mary L Collins, Elmore

Solstice   47
Maria Conti-Reilly, Barre

At the Dentist   48
Ann Cooper, Middlebury

St. Augustine Window
Rhyme or St. Augustine's
Ekphrasis of Light   49
Damian Costello, Montpelier

When Summer Says Goodbye   50
Chad Couto, Stowe

shadow of a crow:
Five pieces for the Year   51
Nichael Cramer, Guilford

Nannie Lee   52
Justin L. Croft, Montpelier

Bits of Icy Clouds   53
Terri Crowther, Washington

"For the Poets"   54
Ralph Culver, South Burlington

A good chance   55
Douglas K Currier, Winooski

Mr. DeJoy, Where are you?   56
daithí, Montpelier

Ages of Rock   57
Sharon Darrow, Sutton

Puppet Master For President   58
Corinne Davis, Montpelier

Locker Room Spirits   59
Greg Delanty, Burlington

April 3rd   60
Chard deNiord, Westminster West

The Migrant Birds   61
Victor Densmore, Hardwick

These weeds, these flames   62
nd dentico, East Montpelier

Reminiscing   63
Elaine Devine, Middlesex

Companion   64
Tristan Devine, Middlesex

Eclipse   65
Monica DiGiovanni, Montpelier

When you were still in
this world   66
Jared Duval, Montpelier

Lament   67
Maggie Eaton, East Montpelier

Politics of Violence   68
Nietzsche Danann Egelanaard, Chelsea

Midwinter   69
Krikmöklet Egelanaard, Chelsea

The First Cherry Blossoms
of Spring   70
Eleanor, age 9

True Love   71
Eleanor, age 15

Loving Is Nice   72
Ellory, age 7

Ordinary Bliss   73
Linda Fialkoff, Fayston

The Size of It   74
Ann Fisher, Lincoln

Dream with Small Familiar   75
Nadell Fishman, Montpelier

At the Library   76
Michael Fleming, Brattleboro

Waiting for Spring's Wisdom   77
Julia H. Fonte, Poultney

Myself to Myself   78
Gary Fox, Barre

The Mighty Moon   79
Lauren Frank, Middlesex

On This Day, January 16, 1605   80
debby franzoni, Castleton

Happy Days Are Here   81
Daisy Freidman, Montpelier

Fezi   82
Frida, age 8

be in touch   83
david fried, Montpelier

With No Feet on the Ground   84
Gaia Fried, Montpelier

Twilight Time   85
Joseph Gainza, Marshfield

This is Our Time   86
Amanda Lucia Garcés, Montpelier

Rhapsody of Flowers   87
Susan Gerretson, Montpelier

Dog Ball   88
Gigi, age 15

Spinning a Yarn   89
brian goodwin, Middlesex

Kinehora   90
Andrea Gould, Plainfield

A Sonnet By An Independent
Woman   91
William Graham, Stowe

The Path of the Orbs 92 Sara Graham, Barre	Chickadee 116 Mary Elder Jacobsen, North Calais
Whirlwind 93 Dave Gram, Montpelier	The Vermont Dream I Woke Up In 117 CurtB Johnson, Calais
Canyon Invocation 94 Gail Grycel, Westminster West	Throwing a Check 118 Daniel Johnson, Winooski
A Solitary Bloom 95 Kathleen Ann Guinness, Poultney	Lola 119 Josephine, age 9
Monhegan 96 Jenny Gundy, Marshfield	what I left behind 120 joy, Montpelier
South Florida Sunrise 97 N.G. Haiduck, Burlington	Thanksgiving 121 Julia, age 10
How to Greet the Evening Star 98 Leigh Gavin Harder, Middlebury	I'm Not 122 Jon Kaplan, Randolph
Kunst Haus Wien (Art House Vienna) 99 Roberta Harold, Montpelier	Intention 123 Beth Kanell, Waterford
keep it simple 100 Neal Harrington, Warren	I See My Mother Fly A Kite In Her Backyard Forty Years Ago 124 Seelai Karzai, Rutland
All About Hannah 101 Hannah, age 7	Before the Redwing Blackbird Sings 125 Monda Kelley, Brandon
Time, You are a Romp in the Backseat, Leaving Me Begging for More 102 Tracy Haught, Duxbury	Melancholy Farewell 126 Jamie Keough, Northfield
Cyclamen 103 Mary E. Hayden, Marshfield	Your Lips Are Like Soft Paws 127 David Klein, Montpelier
You & I at the Cinema 104 Jen Heller, Montpelier	To my daughter on the cusp of her 18th birthday 128 Elizabeth Knapp, East Montpelier
New Year 2025 105 Geof Hewitt, Calais	To Cover the Road 129 Tricia Knoll, WIlliston
Maybe Tomorrow 106 Sam Hewitt, Essex Junction	Sparrow During the Eclipse 130 Phineas Knowles, Bristol
Lake Winona Basket 107 Cindy Ellen Hill, Middlebury	It's the Beginning of the End and I'm Here to Tell You 131 Samantha Kolber, Montpelier
Blue Eyes 108 Angela Hilsman, Montpelier	Aubade 132 AP Kramaric, Winooski
Snow Stories 109 Alicia H. Hingston, Danville	Fogies 133 Luke Krueger, Manchester Center
Breath Divided by Three 110 Lily Hinrichsen, Bristol	Sabrina 134 AB Lafferty, Lyndonville
Over and Under 111 Linda Hogan, Montpelier	An Intent to Commit 135 Bernie Lambek, Montpelier
Epilogue 112 Matt Hollar, Burlington	Queening 136 Jannetta Lamourt, West Dover
Ad Infinitum 113 Stephen J. Holmes, East Montpelier	Watching a Deer drown in the Genesee River 137 Christopher Lawless, Jeffersonville
April 114 Sarah Hooker, Marshfield	Perspective 138 Sydney Lea, Newbury
Rye, 2023 115 J. Lucas Hughes, Montpelier	

Anniversary *Maxine Leary, Montpelier*	139	Leap Year Baby *Maggie McGill, Montpelier*	164
Watching the Enemy Retreat *Michael Levine, Middlesex*	140	exegesis *Becky McMeekin, Braintree*	165
I like... *Liam, age 7*	141	All Giving Oaks *Christine Corrigan Mendez, Burlington*	166
Note to self *Cynthia Liepmann, Middlesex*	142	Finding Nemo *Bob Messing, Montpelier*	167
Coin or Card? *Hugo Liepmann, Middlesex*	143	Pigeon Perspectives *Christy Mihaly, Calais*	168
Snowshoe Hare *Linden, age 12*	144	You are You *Mom, Middlesex*	169
new year *craig line, Calais*	145	Balding Eagle *David Mook, Poultney*	170
Yiayia Gives Gifts of Meli *LN, Fletcher*	146	Did I Think? *Nicola Morris, Plainfield*	171
Fish *Louisa, Grade 6*	147	Comfort If You're Lost *B. Morrison, Brattleboro*	172
How Light Determines a Day *Jesse LoVasco, East Montpelier*	148	Untitled *Kate Mueller, Montpelier*	173
Distraction *Brittany Lovejoy, Montgomery*	149	"The Persistence of Memory" *Giavanna Munafo, White River Junction*	174
Optimism *Luisa, age 8*	150	for the sheer zest of weeds *elizabeth murmuring, Barre*	175
"Friend" *Lydia, age 12*	151	Pernil at Christmas *Barbara E. Murphy, Burlington*	176
Watercolor *Michael Madill, West Topsham*	152	Raising My Spirits *Joan Murray, Worcester*	177
Description of a Struggle *Kimberly Madura, Essex*	153	The Lonely *Michan A. Myer, Randolph*	178
Time *Margo, age 10*	154	Fishing *J.C. Myers, Calais*	179
Flourish *Jack Markoski, Montpelier*	155	A Holy Thing *Erika Nichols-Frazer, Waitsfield*	180
Grief *Lisa Masé, East Montpelier*	156	They Say *nitya, Barre*	181
Show Up *Tamara Mathieu, Swanton*	157	No One Ever Taught Me How To Teach Someone How To Swim *Grady Nixon, Montpelier*	182
Moon *Mayla, age 16*	158	Fable *Penny Nolte, Montpelier*	183
Blessing on the Cow Dreams *Katherine H. Maynard, South Burlington*	159	Belonging to November *Claire Longtin North, Manchester Center*	184
The Sound of War *Tim Mayo, Brattleboro*	160	"mother's eternal blanket" *travis alden stargyll nutting, Middlesex*	185
Wet Wool Mittens *Elizabeth R. McCarthy, Walden*	161	Too Late *Carla (Neary) Occaso, Montpelier*	186
Ardor *Florence McCloud, South Burlington*	162	Bilingual (Japanese/English) Winter Haikus *Michiko Oishi, Montpelier (English translations by Rhea Constantino)*	187
DIstant Friend *JF McGill, Starksboro*	163		

Ten-day silent retreat 2024 188 *Kevin O'Keefe, Brattleboro*	Four Mountain Postures 212 *Charles Rossiter, Bennington*
Car Ride Lullaby 189 *Ann Onymous, Moscow*	Benediction 213 *Sa Sung Ma, Northfield*
Random haikus 190 *Steve Pappas, Plainfield*	Corner poems 214 *Martha Anderson Sanborn, Vergennes*
The Animal Wife 191 *Emma Paris, Putney*	Communication 215 *Sam Sanders, Montpelier*
Today I Was Aglow, So I Made This Poem 192 *Devon Parish, Montpelier*	Queen City Peripheries 216 *Susan M. Sanders, Burlington*
Come Near 193 *Scudder H. Parker, Middlesex*	March Snow 217 *Nancy Scarcello, Florence*
Temperature Rising 194 *Dani Parkins, Essex*	A Conversation Between Friends 218 *Carolyn Cory Scoppettone, Middlesex*
Dreaming of Trees 195 *Annie Perkins, New Haven*	Untitled 219 *Barbara Scotch, Montpelier*
January 196 *Melissa Perley, Berlin*	Mountain Stream 220 *Rachel Senechal, East Montpelier*
Untitled 197 *Jane Pincus, Roxbury*	Window or Aisle? 221 *Angela Shea, Montpelier*
Ferris Wheel 198 *Debra Ann Pinsof-DePillis, Montpelier*	To the Ordinary One 222 *Michelle A.L. Singer, East Montpelier*
tree pose (vrksasana) on Robin's deck 199 *Verandah Porche, Guilford*	Ode to That Picaresque Protagonist Within 223 *sb sōwbel, Montpelier*
On a Mother's Day Hike on Woodbury Mountain 200 *Sean Prentiss, Woodbury*	Reveille 224 *GN Spaulding, Barre*
Scar 201 *Alison Prine, Burlington*	First Harvest 225 *Katie Spring, Worcester*
Breakup! 202 *Parvathi Rajaram, Montpelier*	Summer in Me Heart 226 *Betty St. Laveau, Montpelier*
Sonnet to Save My Life 203 *Kiev Rattee, Manchester*	Rocking Heard 227 *Toussaint St. Negritude, Newark*
Song of the Iris 204 *Susan Reid, Montpelier*	High Holborn Street 228 *Samn Stockwell, Barre*
Snow Is Falling 205 *John Reilly, Barre*	Mooove Towards Justice! 229 *Ashley Anne Strobridge, Montpelier*
Memories 206 *Richard Riley, Montpelier*	gifts from my Father 230 *Karolyn Sudler, Cabot*
To Me 207 *Greg Robertson, Northfield*	Lily 231 *Ananda Oliva Sullivan, Middlesex*
Of Mud and Maple 208 *Andy Robinson, Plainfield*	We live in a world . . . 232 *Geza Tatrallyay, Barnard*
Fries 209 *Roo, age 8*	Solstice Moon 233 *Caroline Tavelli-Abar, Rochester*
Cast Iron Winter 210 *Bruce Jefferson Rose, Monkton*	Once Upon a Time 234 *Tobe Tomlinson, Essex*
I don't 211 *John Rosenblum, Calais*	Rind and Pulp 235 *Evvi Tower-Pierce, East Burke*

The lord is with me and i am trans. *Shawna Trader, East Barre*	236
Rhyme's End? *Robert Troester, Montpelier*	237
Socials *Gina Tron, Barre*	238
Shorn *Tamsen Turner, Albany*	239
Renaistre *Betsy Unger, Montpelier*	240
The Visitor *Nancy Vandenburgh, Milton*	241
Today I Was Extra Sparkly, So I Made this Poem *Emily Walker, Middlesex*	242
Empathy's Crown *Kim Ward, Montpelier*	243
Journeying *Ulrike Wasmus, Calais*	244
Piano Man *Roger Watters, Shelburne*	245
Parking Lot Philosophy *Janet Watton, Randolph Center*	246
May Third *Sharon Webster, Burlington*	247
Socks *T.Wendelken, Montpelier*	248
An Untitled Piece *Zoe Whalen, Montpelier*	249
A Pa's Thanksgiving *CD Williams, Williston*	250
Wolf Moon *Emily A. Wills, Fairfax*	251
Change The Channel *M. Wilson, Barre*	252
Someplace That Will Make the Soul Less Thirsty *Heather Wishik, Woodstock*	253
Thrush Solace *Carl Wrighton, Hyde Park*	254
Buttons *Bianca Amira Zanella, Rutland*	255
This Ash Tree *Zora, age 9*	256
Electrical Hazard *Martha Zweig, Hardwick*	257

PART TWO: **SCHOOLS**

Calais Elementary School *Samantha Jackson's Third and Fourth Grade Class*	260
Main Street Middle School, Montpelier *Kiki Adams' Fifth Grade Class*	270
Main Street Middle School, Montpelier *Debbie Goodwin's Sixth Grade Class*	279
Main Street Middle School, Montpelier *Chrissy Keegan's Sixth Grade Class*	311
Main Street Middle School, Montpelier *Windy Kelley's Fifth Grade Class*	329
Main Street Middle School, Montpelier *Wendy McGuiggan's Fifth Grade Class*	341
Main Street Middle School, Montpelier *Melissa Parker's Fifth Grade Class*	348
Rumney School, Middlesex *Diana Costello's Fourth and Fifth Grade Class*	355
Union Elementary School, Montpelier *Sarah Voorhis' Third Grade Class*	361

Introduction

Is poetry a public or private profession? The poet is a great contradiction in this way. We know—or at least sense—the profound intimacy of poetry: how it manages to touch our inner world, where our most difficult emotions wait to find a voice. What reader of poetry has not had the experience of feeling utterly *seen* by a poem, found in their most intense moments of isolation, and revived by its words. The poem is, as the poet Edward Hirsch said, "the social act of a solitary maker." Poetry demands a public, simultaneously as it demands an individual look inward. This is a time in our world when both introspection and communication are crucial to the survival of our democracy, our culture, or planet. 2025 is a year of great uncertainty, a precariousness unlike we've ever known, and poetry helps give voice to in that instability.

Nowadays, there's no town square where the poet speaks the great stories of the day to the people, though we may gather on wild nights together in the backs of bookstores or bars to do just that. The social touch of poetry is a shadow of what it once was. Yet it's no coincidence that the great epic poems are having their periodical resurgence in the mainstream conversation. These poems were built of an oral tradition of Geek storytellers and song-stitches; when poems *had* to be public to be received. Can we imagine a time when poetry was such an intricate part of society that *everyone* embodied the poems and worked together to keep them alive? We have now, in the Vermont State Capital, our fantastic, valiant version of such public poetry. A city where we can walk down a street and see poetry displayed in businesses and libraries. In our version, we have the language of our intimate lives; we get to see one another as we have not before: our neighbors, friends, colleagues, and strangers. PoemCity is beginning the crucial work of bringing our troubled world back into right relation. This anthology highlights that work, and the collective conversation, which is not just for the few who study poetry professionally. No, with PoemCity we see that even after all these centuries the people still have poetry in their very blood; our innate language; our birthright. Those who choose to engage and share poetry honor that heritage. In this anthology *every* kind of person who engages with poetic form is displayed: all ages, backgrounds, experiences. The novice and the mentor are destined to collaborate in the arc of lyrical communication, and it is a joy to see it here. To hold in my hands. To read it alone late at night, or find it among the city streets.

—Bianca Stone, Vermont Poet Laureate
Brandon, VT

POEMS

a darned shame's antithesis

meets the infinite etcetera,
the black candle longing for an Ohio BlueTip to look its way,
the single red M&M bulging the corner of your envelope,
a crayoned valentine confessional, complete with Xs and Os

silvered circle of light in a darkened theatre,
tattooed on your left palm with invisible ink,
fortuitous as an umbrella's velvet shadow,
astronomical certitude if born in the year of the rat (which i am)

the walking onion loping onto imagination's fertile soil,
a single almond in a pound cake meaning your wish is granted,
a single bay leaf in the sauce foretelling you'll do the dishes,
drowning, the duck's wishbone you snap with both hands

pregnant as a small-town pause . . . intuitive as a swoon,
your lullaby, an angel whisper-singing *the nearness of you*,
in your hand a fresh-picked daisy, one petal left, and . . .
you've just said, "she loves me not."

it's written on the moon in uncertain calligraphy
looky here, look up . . .

—*Rick Agran, Worcester*

Accretion

Each heart, like every chrysalis, must break
to allow transformation.

Like fallow Earth, each must be harrowed bare,

the hard crust of despair broken to embrace new growth.

Awakening, no longer winter seared, until;
In spring-like warmth my heart, now stirring, wakes.
I let the growing beauty guide my feet and, thus faith watered, sing
     my dreams to blooms, in every scent and shade, infused with faith,
     my loving wakes.
Content in knowing, that when at last I fall, my gathered grace returns
     to fertile soil.
For this is love, life undefined by need, born of water, spirit, earth, and Sun.
Through such sweet toil as this is all great beauty bred; passed on to
     fragrant air the blessings pour, to reap from each who pass of dying
     less, and leave for each new life of loving more.

—Alexander and Liam, Montpelier

Morning Dew on a Rose Petal

The water that falls from the sky every day
Tiny little drops blanket the flower petals
The second winter comes that icy chill frozen.
All the water droplets in the sky that gentle morning dew frozen
That used to feel like a warming cloud surrounding you
Now a heavy chill of lonely distance, a sting.
But that warm feeling of hope for the future of a warm morning dew
On a rose petal is still in my mind and i know it will come.

—*Amelie, age 9*

Born

Being human is a guest house.
—Rumi

What sort of thing is a life?
This thing sourced at the whim or plea
of two other lives soon gone,
trundled along pathways undesigned,
tricked into purpose.

What sort of scaffold can a life climb
to look back, to look forward,
to change course, to defy
the promises of importance?
What chance is there to
wink and turn about?

This life will not be gift-wrapped.
Not leached of color,
not offered finally as a cup of dust.
This life will be a wild chant,
sung by a psalm singer in the lion house.
This life will wield a pen racing to
keep up with a mercurial mind.

The rest may be silence.

—*Ina Anderson, South Royalton*
from *Sky Furniture*, Kelsay Books

Looking Up in the Windy Woods

I feel shivers of pain for the trees
   when they creak.
Grrrrrrr noooo,
    they protest
       against the push,
          leaning back against
             the blustering breeze.
Those trees stand straight, sturdy.
solid heartwood. scrappy bark.
   and yet
     and yet
        they bend

—*Cara M.L. Arduengo, Barre*

A mother, A daughter, A child

I feel like I've never stopped grieving a child, a vivid memory that's
    where she stays.
Yet with all the time that has passed I still feel her pain.
I feel her cold tears as they ran down her face.
I feel her frozen fingers and remember how her body trembled partly
    from the snow's icy touch, and her fear.
She gave a jacket to her baby because they were left shivering in their
    summer t-shirt and shorts.
I remember that feeling left in her core.
A pain that felt like a home.
Almost leaving her sour and bitter to the core.
But a sense of hope helped guide her through those treacherous waters.
I will never forget her pain almost numbed by said cold.
I will never forget her determination to protect even when the devil
    stared eye to eye into her soul.
She was a mother, a daughter, and a child with hopes and dreams.
But her heart and soul was like a tarnished silver.
Still good, still beautiful but slowly damaged more and more.
She was a mother, a daughter, and a child.
 Now she is a mother without her children.
She is a daughter resented by her own flesh and blood.
And a child grieving the children she can't hold because at the end of
    the day her children weren't hers And her heart was ripped from
    her body the day they were taken away.
That mother, that daughter, and that child is me and I am her.
 And I hold her dear to my heart.

—Asher, age 17

From Time to Time

The gods can only pray
the prayer of unfolding

that I might know the fiddlehead in spring
becoming fern; the cloud, rain;

the wave on the shore, song;
the myth of the Selkie, the reminder

of the wild beyond the cottage wall,
of my original skin, and the need to return,

from time to time,
to where the prayer began.

—*S. Atwood, East Montpelier*

Blue

Blue looks like ocean waves
Blue sounds like squirtle squirtle
Blue smells like violets blooming
Blue tastes like blueberry plants
Blue feels like stiff stuff

—Augie, age 7

Fiddleheads

Along the roadside
hundreds of fiddleheads,
half-unfurled, huddle
in conclaves of five or six,
solemn heads bowed,
conversing like tiny priests.
Listen—they babble of philosophy
and the arts, of resurrection,
of sniffing muddy streams
and apple blossoms,
talking fast because soon
they will unclench
and become magnificent,
silent peacocks.

—*Charles Barasch, Plainfield*

Astral Projection

I fly overhead for points north
through a clear January night
to consult cosmological beings.
There, my mother is dining with
Carlos Castanada and Don Juan.
She is smiling, her body subtle,
no longer weighted down with all
she lived in life. Carlos and his mentor
are drinking red wine, my mother—
a Diet Coke with ice—her cheeks flushed,
her eyes glowing. They share a secret,
passing it between them like children
in the schoolyard. I am the outsider,
ignored—they are folded into
their amusement of one another.
Tugged back to the earth plane,
I try to shout: Why—When —?
but my words are silenced as
the heaviness descends. I leave
the realm of the wise ones,
to find my questions
lost, no longer salient here,
in the land where influencers prey.

—*Ann Barrett, Marshfield*

Musings From My Paddleboard

What if I didn't live in a no-wake-zone
But instead was luminous and suddenly leapt over the house
Swallowed a star
And painted the sky red
Swung from lover to lover like a trapeze artist just for the thrill of the
    catch and release
Ricocheting from continent to continent
Bouncing from language to language
Then I wouldn't know the little puffs of air as he falls asleep each night
Reaching for my hand
Creases of my palm stained with traces of the garden soil from the
    little furrows I made to plant the carrots that we will savor this fall
Tiny bits of him mixed in the dirt under my nails

—Kathy Barrows, Worcester

Settler

tending / a weak heat
aside the hearth
let it / dissipate
the dry / scorch builds outside
goats / consume brush
flame consumes / what they leave

untouched

sky / knit so close /
thick and heavy
that sun will never / leave
red red orb / still behind eyelids
ash does not / leave lungs

untouched

bake this loaf / in the embers
whole / world
the hearth

—*Julia Barstow, East Montpelier*

a different version of this poem was published in *Dunce Codex*, January 2025

Waves

Before my eyes open
Before the lady clop clops on the boardwalk
Before the builder bangs his nails
My heart has synced
With the rhythm of the waves

Teeming with life
Filling our lives
With glistening sustenance
All you need is a hook

So cast a line honoring
Whatever treasure you reel in
Then fall on your knees
Giving thanks to Neptune
For relinquishing
One life for yours

—J. E. Beatson, Jericho

Dare to Dream

I dare you to dream
Take your aspirations to the extreme

I dare you to soar
Be like an eagle, you will create that door

I dare you to try
Let your limit be the sky

I dare you to see
That you can be anything you want to be

—*Jacqueline Beecher, South Burlington*
from *Walk Through Your Fires*, self-published

Ground's a-Bullin'
homage to David Budbill

Till the soil,
Plant your seeds,
Water well,
Keep out the weeds.

Pick when ripe,
Eat your fill,
Preserve the rest,
Then, just be still.

Stay inside.
Mind the fire.
Wait for Spring.
Nurse your Desire.

—Kim Allen Bent, Montpelier

Listen

Listen
Wait the sound
Closer
It may come
Deep in the night
Slowly rising
Murmur of a song

Here in a quiet place
Voices come and go
Send and reply from all around you
Tales you've heard before

Seeping into every day
The ancient spells
Summoning phantoms where shadows dwell

There's darkness in daylight
Dawn in despair
Doors may open, the way is everywhere

Take these losses, this measure of peace
Carry a question long as a life
Far as it may lead

—Neville Berle, Montpelier

To the Cabinet in the Ladies Bathroom at the Doubletree by Hilton Denver

How weary it must be
for shabby chic cabinetry
in the anteroom of the (Doubletree
by Hilton) ladies' lavatory.

It's next to a cushioned burgundy chair
(no one has ever sat there)
and roughly six feet from where
our inner workings are laid bare.

Why does this cabinet even exist?
Alone in the bathroom, I couldn't resist
verifying each drawer's emptiness.
Then on that theme, I went and pissed.

—Sarah Birgé, Montpelier

Climb

Living in a valley, the main option is up.
The downside being steep walls put the sun to bed early.

No grand sunsets on the horizon,
The valley's edge meeting the sun long before it's ready to set.

Less sun, but more to see.
The land, like a hammock pulled taut, drawing the edges closer,

Fits more in a tight space by building up.
Like skyscrapers of trees, the land has a funny way of mimicking
    cityscapes.

As a valley resident, I climb.
Sometimes more than I brush my teeth, I climb.

To look down at the boxes below,
To see the birds rising up, climbing in their own way.

Like the land around me,
I climb.

—Julia Boles, Montpelier

Fellow Workers

These mornings are juicy
and delicious.
Layers of birdsong pile and push
up a gentle fog.

Apple blossoms pop
outward and punctuate
the unfurling green with
dollops of creamy white.

A fat bumblebee laboriously
fights physics and lunges
from invisible flower to
invisible flower.

This is the world we must labor for,
fight for.
We are fellow workers here:
us, the bees, flowers, birds, leaves.

Singing and opening and tasting
against all odds
to save it all
each morning.

—*Stephanie Boucher, East Montpelier*

Marsh Seasons

January thaw
Almost open waterway
Giving us false hope
Spring rushing water
Cold canoes, warm air, hopeful,
Gleeful, returns life
Summer laziness
Rafting, drifting, fat with peace
Ignore what's coming
Late fall slows and chills
Sticks and leaves, glassy waters
Embracing us all.

—*Rebecca Bowen, Montpelier*

Reaching

Searching for that perfect deep-flavored apple
reaching through orchard's myriad trees
disappointed at flavors mild, overly ripe, sour,
this one mushy, that one hard as a bocce ball

Where is my ideal apple, aroma full and sweet
with juices flowing, flesh yielding yet crisp
deep lingering taste, as complex as my hands
with their multiple bones

I pretend those other fruits ideal—
blueberry, strawberry, raspberry, peach—
and each has its savor, bright and real
as notes of a summer song

But I long for my apple, my apple of depth
with its blush of red, its solid heft

—Anne Bower, South Pomfret

Five Miles from the Fire

It was a spring afternoon
lightly clad young adults
lay near the pond
thinking of nothing
conversing about less.

Five miles away
a spark sputtered, grew hungry
in the bushes
from a careless cigarette
couldn't be seen at first
by cars chugging by,
their occupants open-mouthed,
peering at the pristine pond.

Much later
only barren landscape remained
a lone person
noticed
one blackened sneaker
left behind.

—*Jo Bower, East Montpelier*

The Smell of Fur

I was thinking about the house, that house on the Cape with the creaking of its
haunted stairs, probably. And digging for long-neck clams that had harvested
that ripe boggy smell to leach into the dog's fur. Etched into that moment
when the skiff tipped over and I fell into the cold salt water, shocked into forgetting.

Secondly, in Venice, drunk as a skunk at 3 in the morning. How tipsy I could be in Italian,
I marveled, young and lost to stumble among the canals and narrow passageways that
smelled like the dripping of a wet cave; wandering into the darker dead ends. With the hangover
of an early train ride the next day—so fresh with remorse, who knows what I said?

And the third, that not losing oneself anymore. What's left to lose in that mountain
of voices fading behind me and that distant smell of water? There were so many times
that went on forever, like forever. And I couldn't forget as hard as I tried—like steel.
A casual look from a bird down from a tree reminding me there was more shouting to do.

—Scott Boyd, Stowe

Blue Tarp

Here a Tarp, there a Tarp, everywhere a Tarp Tarp! Did I just start noticing the Blue Tarp? Have we given up, are there no colors left to choose from? I do not like the Blue Tarp!
Is there a Blue Tarp Heaven? Fly away Blue Tarp! I pray it goes there. Got a boat? get the Blue Tarp, got some wood, cover it with Blue Tarp! Oh wait! here are some leaves, get the Blue Tarp.
My neighbors have a family of Tarps, Papa Tarp, Mama Tarp, Baby Tarp, Teen Tarps hanging out! Tots running around with their little Tarp capes pretending to be Super Tarp!
Yaaay! I'm starting to see a plethora of new colors emerging, Brown, Green, Black Tarps, now thats class! Grey Tarp anyone? Lets do grey, grey goes with everything!
Clearly an intervention is needed! Blue Tarp mania smothers my thoughts. With excitement and hope I shall savor this moment as anticipation and delight crowd my imagination with thoughts for a new spectrum of colors!

—Donna Bramley, South Burlington

Molde Beltza

Sump - Pump
Thumps
a wooden echo:
Boots mimicked.
long awaited, never arrived.
Bianchi basement
perennially flooded
deadly mold now our kin.
Only Seasons.
Not people.
Not places.
Remembered now.
Sump - Pump
Always
Thumps.

—*Waters Breedlove, Montpelier*

Anyhow

When I'm not looking, snow begins or ends.
When I'm not looking, the baking sheets slide
in the cabinet, and the dog barks at them.
Someone tucks flyers under windshield wipers,
Secret Santa of the great deal no one wants.
Stickers bloom on signs and poles. "I love you,"
someone crayons on a large blue mailbox.
While I'm dozing, dogs are peeing in snow,
marking poles, linking in to a network.

My parents, miles away, pack their bags for
their next overseas trip, maybe their last.
From down here, I can't see the people borne
in sleek silver lozenges overhead,
their singular faces seeds in the core
of pods designed to sow them far afield.

From most of the seats in an airplane,
the passengers also aren't looking
down at the crazy-quilt earth, or they
want to, anyhow, but can't quite see it.

—*Jenn Brown, Montpelier*

Wings

What words this new year?
New strike new dance new fall.
Color change bright and borne on broken wing beats
dancing between gusts of driven breeze
caught, dropped, and swung low
only to dip
once more
lower
where
half a heartbeat
births breath with wind,
new,
to spiral through
branches green and promise blue

—Mark Brown, Calais

Ireland by Train
(Dublin to Wexford)

behold these
    miles and miles of stone walls
imagine
    hundreds of hands that placed each stone

thousand-year-old placenames
on signposts in Gaelic
whisk past

below in the harbor
wrapped up sailboats rest
                  all dressed in white

security cameras film the pigeons
daffodils rock in unison as the train passes
coffeeshops blink open at dawn
all the windows glow that face the sea
off-leash dogs charge the waves
new lambs sleep beside their kin
and hawks watch from the hazel

—Megan Buchanan, Putney

with stone
　　quiet time
　　deepens

—Cheryl Burghdurf, Middlesex

Dusk

Yellow sunset, baby blue sky:
granite statue of Robert Burns
stands twenty-five feet high
with his back to me—
church steeples
in his line of sight
and a jacket, which he will not need
tonight, in the crook of his arm.
Black darts of birds and
brown bricks, purple trees;
everything set
so it seems
for night and slumber
for dusk to tuck the covers under
and lay to rest
even the best
of schemes.

—wayne f burke, Barre

January Morning

Winter ferns
    bloom in silver arcs
Against the bottle brush of spruce
    high on the black hills turning blue
Turning grey turning white
Below where the sky blushes

—Ana Burtnett, Worcester

Yes, the Duct Tape You Use Matters
NYT, online headline 5/6/23

and today another weird box in the mail, turmeric capsules I never ordered. From a place called H Kreatives, with no web site. Yesterday capsules in an Amazon envelope, immunity boosters. Yes, I'm tired. But who's sending them? I can't think of a single soul. The cosmos? Should Cosmos be capitalized? Last week at the memorial, all these people talking about—well, not heaven, no one used the word heaven, but still a place where Bob is now. An actual place. Hugging his son who'd died young, suddenly, of cardiomyopathy, which my brother has, but he's in his 80s. I guess it's metaphoric. The place. Where you can hold someone in your arms. Tactile. Solid. With walls and windows. And sheet rock. And probably ducts. And this sense that it's not over, that it still matters. Whatever it is. So the duct tape, yes, I guess.

—Sue D. Burton, Burlington

a place inside a place

morning song,
the way branches scrape
against the window,
slowly erasing sleep.

i move equally slow in the early light,
the smell of
wet pavement flowering
inside the air,
a house inside
the house.—

in passing,
the light becomes what it will be:
another day in the abstract of living.—

do you know that every time
we wake, we are coming from
a material place,

a place
inside the place
we dream?-

—*JT Butler, Duxbury*

Chickadees

It was just a small flock, 6 or 8 lively little black and white birds
gathered in the dark spruces and willows on a cold November evening
flitting about low along a partly frozen trickle of stream
conversing buoyantly, as they always do—but this time was different
something about the cadence, the tone, the *excitement* in their voices
What *are* they saying?

Soon it became clear as I watched
one brave little chickadee land at the edge of open water and then
a slight pause, belly flop, splash, shower, spray, flutter, fluff and wriggle
    in seeming delight
then hop out, preen and, by ones and twos, the rest
honor the first and follow to their last bath of the season
before winter's long hard freeze

"We gonna do it?"
"Might be our last chance!"
"Who's going first?"
"If you go I'll go!"
"It's gonna be *cold!*"

I shivered, imagining the lives and the community of these courageous
little beings out here in the unforgiving wild, the unrelenting cold
and with my own delight to witness
such fierce and unexpected beauty

—Barry Cahoon, Danville

Cardinal Love

The soft brown belly of the female at the feeder,
tawny flashing on wings like a whisper,
the blaze of crest and black box face of the male,
demeanor of a startled bishop.
We are not much like these, yet
how naturally and with luck we met,
flight paths turning parallel from different directions,
how we've hopped the same patches of ground,
leapt into the same skies, watching out for each other,
soaring on updrafts, navigating the downs,
pecking for food, braiding twigs into shelter
from storm winds. The delight of shared loves,
the pains and lessons of difference,
the long, continuing flight, destination uncertain and rare,
on separate wings, side by side.

—Dave Cavanagh, Burlington
from *The Somnambulist and the Good Life*, Salmon Poetry

Precious Lives

On a gentle knoll in a small town in rural southwestern Missouri
Lies a treasured family cemetery of the relatives of Felix Burnett.
Felix fought in the Civil War and then died trying to help extinguish a fire
At a neighbor's home in Eureka Springs, Arkansas.
I was drawn into this cemetery on a brisk, sunny morning
as I took my daily walk while visiting my in-laws.
Under a majestic hickory, I reverently began to read the inscriptions
on the graves.

PANSY
July 1905 - June 1906

WELCOM
August 1899 - May 1901

INFANT
INFANT
INFANT

A few more relatives were buried alongside these small headstones,
But my heart broke to think of the tragedy that was faced with each and every
death of these babes and infants.
I sat on a bench inscribed "In Loving Memory of Our Mother"
and sent prayers and
Love to the rural townsfolk whose lives were so deeply touched
by this sadness and grief.
Tears streamed down my cheeks as I resumed my walk and headed home
To the loved ones of my husband's family,
Under the watchful eyes of the herds of curious cows, with long lashes.

—Susan Chickering, East Montpelier

What is a Flower

A flower is a plant

A flower has petals

A flower could be a lion's mane swishing in the breeze

A flower could be a night star in the sky

A flower could be the sun

A flower could be anything

If you use your imagination

—Chloe, age 8

Desire Lines

You're not supposed to go that way
but that's where you go.
Down the path of least resistance
like a dog following its nose.

Learning they have a real name,
desire lines, I see them everywhere.
A guilt pang when I take one, but
I'm just following the crowd.

You've seen them, haven't you?
Soft trails between college towers,
or the de-grassed ground
arrowing to a riverside.

They tempt you: a second saved
here and there, turns
into a couple minutes
you'll savor at the end of your life.

—*Alice Christian, Colchester*

At the Core

Spirits are alive with vibrant colors I only see
With my eyes closed?
A fluorescent truth that cannot be erased
From any cave wall?
I taste the grit of a city in every dream
An art on the inside?
Blueberry flavorings mixed with people
Projected in shadows?
What hidden messages bring revelation
Tonight, through nostrils?
What haunted looks tell a story of pain
Never shared?
Will salvation come in the darkness
So melancholy?
I hear the trees sing a precise possible
Way forward?

But the radiance of a creative point of existence
Takes me into a depth no one can ever weigh,
Or measure, or feel,
And I am here or there, or maybe everywhere,
At the core.

—*Peter L Clark, Woodbury*

Storms Outside and Inside

Today I did not leave the house.
It was cold outside and inside was not much better.
The cold creeps in from the cracks between us.
You see me as a burden, but I see you as burned out.
Looking out the window snow drifts across the yard.
It is blowing the flag like a surrendering ship.
You are a sinking wreck battered by life's storms.
I need a lifeboat.
The spring will come before we know it.
I hope to bloom with the melted snow as the sun warms the earth.
I will leave this house.
See me drift away.
I will be rescued.

—*Conor Isaiah Cleveland, Williamstown*

Ode to Spring

One mild day after winter ran off
we ventured out
the dogs and I quietly
in a field of thawing
spongy ground
our three heads
slowly and carefully looking
thicket to river and bramble to bank
hoping for small hopping
flying and budding things.
Birds, chipmunks, snakes, swollen red twigs—
the ten-thousand wonders of April.
Wiping winter white
from our eyes and
in the company of sparrows
we loudly sang our ode to Spring.

—Micki Colbeck, Strafford

In and Out of the Cold

Morning May, its dreams are almost gone—
I'm buried in a thick black-currant dark.
                Sun crawls along the birch's crackling bark.
                The early calling birds are all still yawning.
Two dodgy dogs, a blur, rush out to do
a greeting peed upon the patchy snow—
                this message, color of a pale noon glow,
                is answered as red trilliums break through
the day, obstetric moment of a spring,
when limbs and heads are crowning.
                Ferns uncurl, the crocus stalks're breaking.
                Daffodils arise, like gold-crowned kings.
An army bearing gray-green spears aboil,
the peonies swelled pregnant buds set fast,
                exploding into multicolored globes so vast
                they shudder from the flower to the soil.
A brief catch-breath, our northern vernal day
—with kiss so deep its heat endures till May.

—PH Coleman, South Burlington

Apples on The Shelf
Martha's Kitchen 1969

Martha didn't like help with the cooking,
I was the one who set and cleared the table,
and watched.

I watched apples get old
sitting on the kitchen shelf.
Why Mart wouldn't throw them away,
I just couldn't understand.
Their redness and shine
turned brown and wrinkled.

I remember handling the apples,
each covered with its own greasy wax.

First she made a crust
with lard and all-purpose flour.
One by one, Martha carefully peeled and sliced each apple.
She added cinnamon, sugar and lemon juice.
Just before the final, pierced crust,
she dotted pats of butter all over the top.
Once the pie was baked, I will never forget

that from those old, brown apples came
the very best apple pie I had ever eaten.

—*Carol Johnson Collins, South Duxbury*

the one about johnny spaniel

for hayden carruth

I read your poem this morning—the one about johnny spaniel. It reminded me of my grandfather, your voice, similar. I would sit at his feet listening to him tell stories in that thick, cadenced Vermont drawl, the one that sounded like syrup on pancakes, the one none of us could ever have had too much of. It was a voice as sticky as jam, a song sweeter than a prayer, a story metered out like butter on bread. Like your poems, his voice was plumb. I can hear you say it—"plumb", the way few things are these days, the way I feel reading your words, or better still, hearing you read them yourself, how you captured us, straight and true, how you sincerely loved who we are, how we came to be just this way—rough, sturdy, squared off, with an honest lack of pretense that shows up in the way we say "bi knock lee ars", or how we know the seasons by scent, how to find our way home just by scanning the lay of the land, finding the one familiar tree, a sentinel deserving of our gratitude, not to be cut for firewood. we're still standing, some of us an'aways. I see glimpses of us in the woman who cuts my hair and talks about hunting, "We don't get lost in the woods," she says, as she snips my bangs. "It's how you know a local from a flatlander." I miss that about this place.

I miss the voices that speak true, the ones that know the guideposts, never get lost. Not at the IGA, not in the deep woods of Sterling Valley, nor in a room full of strangers who insist that we mingle. Since when did Vermonters ever mingle? I miss that you're not here among us to swap stories of farmers, and n'er-do-wells like us, of beauticians who hunt and know their way around the woods as easily as they do a cowlick. There are just a few of us left, holding on to what you once taught in your poems. I'm grateful you listened as closely as you did, wrote it all down, made words plumb. I'd still recognize your voice, if I were to hear it again, somewhere among all the migrations, through poverty, death, and climate change, and all that goddamn political wrangling. You would be standing here among us, a take-no-prisoners backwoods archangel, pen in hand, honest dirt under your nails, reminding us of who we once were and who we might, still, become.

—Mary L Collins, Elmore

Solstice

Beneath this cloud encumbered
moonless night wails a breathless song.
Burning fingers seek comfort,
curling in a tribal toe numbing crouch—
We huddle shoulder to shoulder
all heads intent on this task
collecting our desire in this stone-lined well;
round, broad, embracing our potential,
deep enough to cradle this
archaic errant spark of hope.

—Maria Conti-Reilly, Barre

At the Dentist

Relax your shoulders, Ann,
unclench your hands.
Close your eyes and see
the intensity of a lover's face, feel
the warmth and pressure of the clasp of hands.

Eyes open once again take in,
through the window facing you,
the sticks of leafless trees
against a fall-blue sky,
clouds drifting toward a future
shortened with each breath.

—Ann Cooper, Middlebury

St. Augustine Window Rhyme or St. Augustine's Ekphrasis of Light

Around the church, not too far
Walk with Jesus, Morning Star
Chant with us, keep the time
St. Augustine Window Rhyme
Golden crown and nine stars that shine
Temple Presentation time
Cherubim on the Ark
Kings find Jesus in the dark
Temple gate, David's Throne
Family finds Egypt home
Snake around a silver ball
Boy in Temple teaches all
Castle with the guards of Rome
Shell with drops that brings us home
Baptized, Holy Ghost they see
Alpha, omega, eternity
Jesus shining on the hill
Elijah, Moses standing still
Anchor then three waves of blue
Lazarus lives anew
Machete then a rich young man
Globus cruciger in hand
Angel Choirs praise the Lord
St. Michael with a flaming sword

—Damian Costello, Montpelier

When Summer Says Goodbye

When the summer says goodbye
And the trees begin to cry
And the ground turns hard
Underneath a November sky
And all the light once given
Will seep away
Making way for darkness
That fills the shrinking days
The empty branches creek and groan
An eerie lament
The whispers from the vibrant leaves
Have long been spent
The memories of summer time;
A cloak against the cold
Yet dead upon the ground
The leaves that trees did hold
Contracting from the chilling touch
The cold too much to bear
The tingling smell of change;
A strong perfume of deep despair
A grave tomb frozen world
Under a gray canvased sky
A world transformed by winter
When summer says goodbye.

—Chad Couto, Stowe

shadow of a crow: Five pieces for the Year

Surely no sane man
Would travel to Cold Mountain
—Make yourself at home

                        dark of night
                        touching the shadow
                        of a crow

warm winter evening
I clear
my browser history

                                —With Zhang Zi
                        Waking at dawn
                        I can't wait to see
                        who's that dancing outside my window.
                        butterflies
                        on a sunlit field
                        or a million snowflakes on the wind.

Raven pretends
he doesn't see me
either

—*Nichael Cramer, Guilford*

previously published, respectively, in *Tricycle*, January 2024; in *bottle rockets 25.2*; in *Frogpond*, Spring 2024; in *bottle rockets 25.0*; and in *Nor'easter*, October 2024

Nannie Lee

I want you to know
that I see you

filling the salt shakers
wiping down the tables
muttering
in rhythm
to yourself

you might be the most
invisible person
in this room of hundreds

but to me
you're the only one
in color

—Justin L. Croft, Montpelier

Bits of Icy Clouds

Bits of icy clouds fall, creating
A pathway from sky to earth
Covering the remnants of autumn
With a blanket of winter calm

Bits of icy clouds fall, creating
A pathway of snowflakes that turn
Lawns to diamonds in the sunlight
Trees to shadows in the moonlight

Bits of icy clouds fall, creating
A pathway of visitors' calling cards
Pointed hoofs heading to the apple trees
Circular paws emerging from the barns

Bits of icy clouds fall, creating
A pathway of boot prints to the wood pile
Glenwood stoves heating our soup
Hearths warming our soul

—*Terri Crowther, Washington*

"For the Poets"

You are reeling fish
out of the air

whether you are willing
or not

You keep doing it

It is appeasement

It is not helping much

Any

But
as the acorn is the oak's fortress

as the egg is the descent
the bird makes
seeking to rise

though there are no fish

you know they are there

—Ralph Culver, South Burlington
previously published in *On the Seawall*, November 2024

A good chance

There's a good chance it was all a mistake
—driving away all those afternoons beer by beer,
wanting so much so much faster, Marlena.

Adolescence—a fast river you step into
and immediately lose your balance.

Current tossed, you don't remember taking
that step, making any sort of decision at all.

Too wet to ever be comfortable—the landscape
changes every damn time you come up for air.

Live fast . . . ? Is there any other way?

Adulthood is a rock-strewn beach,
and you still don't know where you are.

—Douglas K Currier, Winooski

Mr. DeJoy, Where are you?

to Ben Doyle & others for getting our P.O. back
& to the local postal carriers who delivered over time

No one sends me letters anymore.
Even the P.O. Master tends to ignore me.
Perhaps I'm barking up the wrong door.

What is the point of writing for?
Most notes are sent by computer. I'm forlorn.
No one sends me letters anymore.

I miss our local P.O.—what it stood for.
It got swept downriver to god-knows-where.
Perhaps I'm barking up the wrong door.

I've written to the P.O. Master to implore
Him to return our P.O. and restore it.
No one sends me letters anymore.

While you may think me a complete bore,
I'lll still ask for time on the public floor,
Perhaps I'm barking up the wrong door.

—*daithí, Montpelier*

Ages of Rock

Rock-
a-bye,
rock 'n' roll,
Rock of Ages,
my life volcanic
in geologic time.
Oceanic mountains brought
downstream, broken in ice, in rain,
mountains to hills to boulders to rocks,
pebbles to sand underfoot in the brook.

I gather loaf-sized rocks to line gardens,
climb boulders, trail toes in cold water.
Stillness on silence, dark fish hide,
water surface their ceiling.
Tiny water striders
make surface tension
their floor, humans
no more than
weather,
stone.

—Sharon Darrow, Sutton

Puppet Master For President

I awoke this morning dreading that he had won. I didn't turn on the television or
Radio, as I didn't want to hear the buzz of victory. Instead I looked at my phone
and felt instantly defeated and ashamed. "How could this be, why can't the rest
of the Country see what I see?"

I hungered to win, to convince myself that I am right, to put myself at ease, so
that I can close my eyes when I sleep, avoiding nightmares of loved ones being
executed. I want to remain in denial, that our Country is a safe place, rather
than accepting, that the corrupt can buy their way to the Presidency.

Oh yes, Satan is President once again, masterfully, manipulating his pawns. He
gleefully plays with his puppets, as they jump to his every whim. Helplessly, they
cower in fear, as if, at the hands of the Mafia, while he slowly builds his
dictatorship on false promises.

We are no longer the United Nations.

—*Corinne Davis, Montpelier*

Locker Room Spirits

for Vine Crandell and in memory of Pat Cavanagh

On a high, the combo of relief my daily lap-regimen
    at the pool was done and the ensuing lift
(the endorphin charge that exercise injects within,
    the body's hit of happy drugs, nature's gift)
has me jest with another Y old-timer, about our cancers.
The biopsy scar-tissue, still fresh on Vine's shoulders,

reminds me of Pat's melanoma, his winning resistance
until a second cancer ambushed him: my manly kind.
Besieged on all sides, he fought the spreading advance
    with counter-attacks of chemo, only to find
himself caught in the crossfire. He tried. He died,
a noble victim of the cancer wars, none more dignified.

I tell myself think survivors: Adrie, Tom, Gerry, Marie, Jen.
Shake that sinking feeling. Maybe time for a lap swim again.

—Greg Delanty, Burlington

April 3rd

There is a new quality in the air:
a sweet redolence from the first flowers
and pungent odor in the soil emerging
from the thaw, that smell that spring passes
under your nose to wake you again,
more than wake you, stir you in such a way
that you recall the irony that *kills*:
the shadow in the drupe, the upswing
on the ward.
      How strangely and there-
fore divinely your mind suddenly turns
in its thinking of your soul as a cloud
that assumes a panoply of mystical forms,
including a Chinese mirror in which your body
suddenly appears as a vast array of creatures:
ant, trout, hawk, gazelle and so on.
You laugh and a flower blooms beside
a door in a meadow that opens onto
a darkness so deep no light can pierce it.
That is the zero by which everything
in the world is multiplied at dusk.

—Chard deNiord, Westminster West

The Migrant Birds

They will not forsake us
nor disappoint everlong,
but will appear in their own good time
always to our wonder and delight.
And of our friends, who down the years
have shared with us
these rites of Spring and Fall,
the memories are beautiful and bittersweet.

—*Victor Densmore, Hardwick*

These weeds, these flames

I come armed with weeds
Against those that fear the invasion of life
I come armed with weeds
Because folks are hungry while there is food all around.

I come draped in the flames of serrated leaves
Not to attack.
Not for offence.

But for the dangerous hope that lurks deep inside us all that there might be a path forward through these stinking walls of control and concrete that keep these weeds from creeping up through; that the concrete won't keep these flames from rising out of the footprints of the colonizers (who must always be watching their backs); faith that these leaves will return again each spring to feed the folk.

I come armed with weeds
Because I love you even though you are different and maybe you don't have the right number of petals or your stems aren't smooth enough or your leaves aren't alternate or your stamens are in different places or you grow in the shade.

I come armed with weeds.
Let's eat.

—nd dentico, *East Montpelier*

Reminiscing

Age comes to us
slowly at first,
then steady,
predictable.

Stories of what once was,
trailing conversation.

I'd rather discuss
the tug
on my soul,
with the sun's daily appearance.

I'd rather walk the coyote's
footprints.

Follow the deer's trail.

Feel the earth
carry me,
forward.

A being,
in this universal moment.

—*Elaine Devine, Middlesex*

Companion

The mundaneness of our morning walk is not lost on me.
Yet in the mundaneness, you never fail to be amused.

I trade you safety
and you gift me—
a sense of wonder.

—*Tristan Devine, Middlesex*

Eclipse

September 18, 2024

Walking the neighborhood
under a bright full moon eclipse.
My footsteps gently echo
a boundless, starry night.

Canopy of trees, the pause of darkness
overburdened by lamplight.
Startled by hooves tapping pavement
we meet eye to eye.

Reticent young deer looks back
before being consumed
by its forest sanctuary.
Where is the rest of the herd?

Alone by the tree,
where it was snacking on just-ripe apples,
one drops into the grass by my feet
with a surprisingly audible thud, saying, "Hey you?"

It bounces to the sidewalk,
then wobbles downhill, into the gutter.

—*Monica DiGiovanni, Montpelier*

When you were still in this world

Today I shoveled the snow off the back porch steps.
Underneath were hundreds of needles,
Fallen from the Christmas tree you helped me
Drag outside and put in the back of your truck.

The smell of evergreen was still fresh,
A time capsule of the day you died.

I bent down and put my face on the steps,
Crouching until my knees were wet,
Trying to relive what it was like
When you were still in this world.

The morning after you died, I had hesitated to shower.
Your scent, of wood smoke and work, was still on me.
From kneeling on the floor next to your body
My tears falling on your cold face, while holding your hand,
And telling you I love you, and that
I hope to be even half the Father you were.

After a pause, I stepped under the water
Realizing that
My blood is your blood,
And flesh is far more lasting than a scent.

—Jared Duval, Montpelier

Lament

I heard the loon call and call again
For the first time this blistering,
searing summer
Pleading, plaintively, mournfully
Its tragic yearning tone
Bordering the stillness
Expelling air with flattened feathers
Gliding, drifting
Plumed and ready
To plunge solid-boned
Into starless water
Accompanied by silver slaps
of lake waves
Keeping eternal time

—*Maggie Eaton, East Montpelier*

Politics of Violence

The head
Does what it wants
While the hands do the work
And starts fights not with a punch but
A nod

—*Nietzsche Danann Egelanaard, Chelsea*

Midwinter

The night we fill dark like scavenging animals
Some long-fingered, bushy-tailed reveries, we
crush crustaceans scarved in pomme wood-smoked bacon and
plates of chèvre-stuffed endive, sweet with pomegranates

Black night, longest night, fires burn inside in iron
hog bellies against the cold, brittled windows glow
half caked under snow, and jump-ups sleep their roots to
sally themselves to that bland host, temperate time

Warm and cool colored auras halo small lights of
a tall pine, broad, straight, and handsome in his temple
shrine—the flickering candles, the twinkling ice strands,
and cauldron of endless hibernal libations

Anniversary: the birth of Sol Invictus
Happy, indomitable crowing of the sun
Gifts of heart we offer his crowning chariot
'cross the star-drenched cosmos through to summer solstice

To red cherries laid on red linen; blood and bones
of the bull, and happy clattering of spoons and
bowls, and pansy eyes beaming triumphant of frosts
And each warm body singing blithely, Sol Sol Sol!

—*Krikmöklet Egelanaard, Chelsea*

The First Cherry Blossoms of Spring

I Hear The Lovely Bird Song
I Taste The Sweet Nectar Of The Cherry Blossom
I Feel Calm As I Inhale The Scent Of The Cherry Blossoms
I See The Luscious Pink Cherry Blossoms On The Trees In The Park At
    The Festival In Japan

—*Eleanor, age 9*

True Love

The love of a father
Loving His child
Close as a friend
In the times of hard trials
A love unfathomable
A love so dear
One that stays close
One forever near
It's strong like a mountain
It doesn't fear the landslide
Abundant as a fountain
For you in it to abide
Something everyone wants
So free and so full
Something everyone needs
To be and to pull
To pull on to the finish line
A finish line of peace
One you can hope for
May not come with ease
But it's forever worth it
An eternity of reward
To have a home in Heaven
With our loving Lord

—*Eleanor, age 15*

Loving Is Nice

Loving
Oh, how much fun
Valentines
Every kind can love

Impossible to stop doing it
So nice

Nice, Kind, Loving!
It is great to be loving
Cycle of Love
Everything can love

—Ellory, age 7

Ordinary Bliss

Inside I tend to clothes:
hiss of steam iron on linen.
Wrinkles turn smooth and crisp
under damp heat./
Click-clack of sewing machine:
patching these ancient jeans,
hoping to get more life from
fabric that has given its best./
Outside torrential rains still.
Pulling on boots, I step out
into sopping clover, stoop
to pick wild strawberries./
Rain resumes a softer song.
Drops by the thousands
pattering the pond
in hypnotic rhythm./
Later, back inside
I remove wet clothes,
inspect clean sheets
with profound gratitude./
I awaken from dreaming
blessed by sound sleep.
In the numinous deep,
I am made new again.

—Linda Fialkoff, Fayston

The Size of It

hate is a hole so vast
even nothing can't quite fill it

so flammable the fire of thought
consumes its everything

searing us unrecognizable

concealed, we carry fear
misnamed protection
tainted by its gamey glow

no life-slice left
untouched
leaving shrunken-appled hearts

and minds so dwindled
against the pressure
of collective loathing

even the fruit fly
appears gargantuan

—Ann Fisher, Lincoln

Dream with Small Familiar

We talked last night
in a dream. You gave me
sage advice, but now
I can't remember what it was.
Such are the faulty hours
 between sleep and waking.
When we met you had a terrible
haircut, as if the groomer
saw you as a punk rocker,
and blunt cut your white hair
up and down and all around
your small Westy body.
I loved you immediately and you
meticulously licked my face,
as if you already knew
we were made for each other.
Jump ahead the twelve years we lived
 together and the years since you've been gone.
We have a big girl in the house now.
She's a golden doodle three times your size,
as you probably know.
I visit your stone every spring, summer
and fall day. She comes, too,
and likes to sniff around your grave.

—*Nadell Fishman, Montpelier*

At the Library

It happened at the library—a book
was in my lap, the words were songs, the air
was made of light, and everywhere I looked

was glass, dancing plasma, cool to the touch
and smelling like raspberries. When I took
a breath, my eyes began to see with such

clarity and connection, peace and prayer,
the undiscovered knowledge of so much
more—at the library, our anywhere.

—Michael Fleming, Brattleboro

Waiting for Spring's Wisdom

Winter's trees threw off
   their coats of color
to show their true selves
   and the stories of their lives.
The sky has rained gaping
   wounds into their bellies,
wind and elusive sun
   have twisted their arms,
and lightning has broken
   their bones, maybe their spirits
or my heart, having
   grown with them for so long.
But resilience is their mainstay,
   one of mine, too,
while they wait for new buds,
   and I prepare to renew
as we live the life
   we all have been given.
Nudging their roots deeper
   as I dig within,
they stand taller each year,
   and with a gift of grace
perhaps I become a bit wiser.

—*Julia H. Fonte, Poultney*

Myself to Myself

Ugly
Stupid
Worthless
Crazy

From morning to night
From childhood to adulthood
My value defined externally
I could not see the diamond in me

I internalized the words and carried on the work
This family scapegoat believed every lie
Praise deflected, self-worth undetected
All abuse earned, no kindness deserved

Unaware of my noble mission
Darkness seemed my eternal prison
I wasted away, drunk and decayed
Till I saw my reflection and began my self-correction

I was lied to but I will not lie to myself
I will fix what needs fixing
I won't fix what isn't broken
I'll check my mirror from morning to night

—Gary Fox, Barre

The Mighty Moon

Amidst the purple glow of dusk, before the sun settles in the west
She appears as a ghost of herself, the moon ready to manifest.

She lifts her silvery gaze to the darkening space above
Biding her time as she rotates into the setting she loves.

From center stage in the sky, now blanketed in black
The stars awake and brightly shine, welcoming her back.

She calls to all the creatures of the night
Eyes aglow with the nighttime gift of sight.

The ocean tides feel her tug like a warm embrace
Moving in familiar rhythm with natural grace.

Like a spell cast, many are summoned to Dreamland
A place of peace, fright, or something perfectly grand.

Whether she sits amongst a clear sky or angry storm
She is always there, providing, no matter her form.

She is the Mighty Moon, her influence and pull never ending
The night is hers to command, magic and surprises impending.

—Lauren Frank, Middlesex

On This Day, January 16, 1605

the first modern novel, *Don Quixote*,
by Miguel de Cervantes, was published

and with it its star, Alonso Quixano,
a man on a horse, slow

or in full gallop, he became a swashbuckler
who roamed La Mancha in Spain,

taking on un seen foes, tilting at windmills,
his quest to dream the impossible dream.

It seems human beings are forever
the same, arriving from infinite smallness

to grow to disclaim everything
that appears magical

until the day of surrender content,
a slight smile as daylight winks

from behind—it was all a dream
then flashes ahead.

—debby franzoni, Castleton

Happy Days Are Here

Beyond the clouds
The happy sun smiles.
Still is the air.
Not one bird sings.
Suddenly, Mr. wind blows.
A patch of blue appears.
The whole sky is blue.
The happy son is laughing.
The birds sing again.

—*Daisy Freidman, Montpelier*

Fezi

I see my dog Fezi when I get home. I hear Fezi's bark as I come back from the movies. I smell the shampoo at Petco. I feel like I could taste treats that are Fez's. I feel Fezi's love for me.

—*Frida, age 8*

be in touch

there is a plant in hawaii called "sleeping grass"
when i bend down to touch it
it curls up its leaves
as if to say
"brother, i can't take it anymore"
but how do we know
if it is really crying out to be touched?
it expresses its joy by folding up
into a smile
but since i am not a plant
i can only imagine what it is feeling
it has no idea of why i am reaching to touch it
so it waits
and when i stroke its soft leaves
it slowly folds up
and stays that way for awhile
that feeling of being appreciated
vibrating in its stems
a link between the people and the plant world
humming to us if we listen
"be gentle"
"be kind"
"be a good friend"
"be in touch"

—david fried, Montpelier

With No Feet on the Ground

I maneuver my 12' ladder
between the crumbling wooden structures that used to display plants
and the trunks and branches of the 40 year old kiwi vines.
Squeezing up trees, steps, and the coils of this Jack in the Beanstalk
I shut my eyes and go by feel: If I look, I'll see it's not possible

On top of the ladder,
faint from heat and humidity,
glasses fogged, sweating through my T shirt
I let go of my father's equipment
and entangle myself into the vine.

My head has bent back reaching for kiwis so long
I forget reality, forget where I am, forget to hold on.
I can't listen to audio books;
one second musing about the Russian Revolution, and I'll let go
A sound from behind could knock me off, the thud of an apple

I am wondering all day,
If I fall, will the vine bend and give and stretch to save me?
Or will it snap?

I picked my weight in kiwis this summer.
The magic fell to earth.

—Gaia Fried, Montpelier

Twilight Time

When in the brightness of a sunny day
our spirits lift as the living earth reaches up and out
when the darkness we too often associate with badness
        is overcome
we see so clearly the surface of things.
The sounds of living intensify
        the doves coo, the branches rattle
and become the vocal cords of the wind.
Our minds race in awe and wonder over the hills
and into the hearts of flowers   and the flight of the hawk.
Nature is on the move and calling on a sunny day.
We open to the familiar and friendly world
        with gratitude and hope.
The earth turns away from the sun, the light deepens
and gentle winds pull the curtains
        over the surrounding world.
Twilight pays too brief a visit yet in that time
what has been just below the surface emerges.
The inner world becomes more explicit—enchantment
succeeds gratitude and justifies hope
stories are born and coalesce   into life enhancing narratives.
In twilight time the Spirit of the world
whispers the song of life and its
        journey home.

—Joseph Gainza, Marshfield

This is Our Time

This is our time to come together.

When they say you are a criminal,
> When they say you are only a man or a woman and nothing else,
> When they say you don't belong,
> When they say you are not like them,

When they say—
> You do not have their intellect, You do not have their dollars,
> You do not have their inheritance, You do not have their backbone—

We say:

This is our time.
> Who we are is—Love, Community, Peace, Strength.

What we have is *us*.

We are abolitionists.
> We are multi-spirit.
> We belong.
> You belong.

This is our time—
> The revolution of love.

—Amanda Lucia Garcés, Montpelier

Rhapsody of Flowers

In the starkness of winter, not knowing what is to come,
Our palette is darks and whites with muted colors timidly appearing,
Too cautious to boldly reveal themselves.

Spring arrives and from the underground arise valiant stalks of life,
Persistent in striving to awaken both themselves and those around,
Hoping to recruit all those who will rise to join the Spring.

Spring flowers will blossom more tentatively upon their awakening,
They tend to be more careful exploring their environment,
Strength is slowly building among their own kind.

Eventually, a vast array of flowers will arrive as the days warm,
They may be more reluctant to join the ranks of other flowers,
Some may have discordant colors to their own, with no signs of harmony.

Suddenly, the day will come that they form a rhapsody of flowers,
All colors and varieties, fragrances, and life stages present,
Buds, fresh blooms, and fading flowers each add their notes to the music.

This lush symphony of these brave soldiers who strive to glorify,
Nurtured by warm summer days and stalwart rain, will fade into the fall,
To dream in the winter night with plans to rise again.

—*Susan Gerretson, Montpelier*

Dog Ball

asteroid crater like a dog bowl
wagging and skipping
hopping like a diamond skin snake on tickled moonshadows
there is no grace below the last dirt horizon
frozen to the touch by a cosmic kernel, straight outta the pot
there is
—only a whim, buoyant and distant
from slow dripping of chantilly lace down perfect plaster
only a smile, jaw tingling and heart-breaking
the gentle goodbye rings of january
only the kaleidoscope dip+twist dance of living things
souls like ribbons, or blurred film
—don't ask me if snakes can dance, rocks themselves dance
flying and crying white hot veiling tears
to the open earth, you settling with a
BOOM
to weep smush eyed and heavy
between the smile and the shoulder
while the jubilant dog barks with the laughing stars

—*Gigi, age 15*

Spinning a Yarn

when you were young up before dawn
mama would knit
while you pulled the yarn

trying to keep up
after her yarn bunched up
many times she tried
but her pattern was gone

putting her knitting down
time went on
lifting you up and putting you down

fed you so well
made sure you had all
everything you needed so you could cast on

you now sit up late
never hesitate
a thread, a stitch, knitting and purling
spinning a yarn

up until dawn, hard to put down
lucky to have a string to hold on

—brian goodwin, Middlesex

Kinehora*

When things were going well,
I embraced my big life,
layering gratitude on rice paper
and folding it like origami
into a thousand poems.
I imagined the spirits
were waiting for me
to spit three times,
say Kinehora,
throw salt over my left shoulder,
and find some wood to knock on.
Now I wonder if there is enough
salt in the Dead Sea,
enough wood in the Redwood Forest,
and enough spit
in our throats
to intone Kinehora

—*Andrea Gould, Plainfield*
*kinehora: Yiddish expression meaning to ward off the evil eye

A Sonnet By An Independent Woman

I am a voluntary refugee
From romance. My singular self sustains
My life just fine. Masculine company
Is about as welcome as acid rain.
My intellect is as sharp as my wit.
On my walls hang prestigious diplomas.
To someone less learned I will not commit.
Stupid men exude a rank aroma.
I've made my own way in this nasty world.
I manage my large stock portfolio.
Precious independence I have preserved.
Frankly, I am rich. I don't need a beau.
With lady friends I'll jet to the Maldives
To savor sun, sand, and ocean breezes.

—*William Graham, Stowe*

The Path of the Orbs

The dark orb of the MOON shrouding the sun
Yet encircled with its glowing halo
Casting a shadow over this one sliver of our aqua and emerald sphere

Here among the silhouette of the trees etched against the fading twilight
We witness the aligning of these three spheres in their gravitational gavotte
Creating this darkening of the day

For one ephemeral moment we stand in this penumbra
Beholding the balancing of the spheres
Knowing we, this speck of humanity are here, embers of the universe

—Sara Graham, Barre

Whirlwind

From the start of Hollywood films
In the teens and early twenties,
They glamorized the car
Until by '25, it had become
The object of mass desire

By '40, they'd built
The Pasadena Freeway
Free, they said,
Because it would come without cost.

By the '60s, The Beach Boys were singing
Of Little Deuce Coupes and 409s.
From the "Love Bug" to "Mad Max," no city more promoted
The internal combustion engine.

By the 1970s, L.A. had the worst smog in the country.
And still, in the '90s, they laughed off some Adirondack hermit
Who wrote about "The End of Nature."

When '25 rolled 'round again, the city was ablaze
And somebody somewhere
Searched Google for the phrase,
"Reap the whirlwind."

—Dave Gram, Montpelier

Canyon Invocation

When the cunning coyote
whispers in your dreaming ear,
May the ancient language
only you remember lead
you into the canyon's cave,
where the ancestral souls speak
in riddles and metaphors, where
in the stillness you already know,
only you can battle the haunting
creatures shrouded within your shadows.

May the sculpting wind wrap
its caressing wings around your spirit,
slipping over crumbling stone,
filtering through the creek's dripping trickle,
and shift under the silky desert sand—
when you, luminous
against the ravine's sunlit rim,
blend with essence, and being, and root.

—Gail Grycel, Westminster West

A Solitary Bloom

On Owl's Head, a small mountain in Maine,
We found, to our great wonderment,
A single, tiny, delicate Pink Lady's Slipper,
Growing on, of all things, a lichened rock,
A flower known for its roots seeking wetness
In deciduous forests.

Our minds filled with questions,
We descended the steps of the mountain,
To continue our trek on Earth,
A solitary bloom in itself
Among millions of others,
But one that has been miraculously pollinated
As if by bees, and thrived through
Centuries of questioning minds,
Not unlike ours,
Pondering the existence of a solitary Lady Slipper
On Owl's Head.

—Kathleen Ann Guinness, Poultney

Monhegan

One mind is floating out to sea
to a place where eiders climb
seaweed draped rocks
and snooze in the sun.
Fog shrouded thickets
drip with birds in the morning
darting among cone clad treetops
snatching flies from the air.
Borne on air currents up the Atlantic coast
they hear water exploding against rock
fall out of the sky
and paint the scrubland
with blue, yellow, orange, black, and green.

Another mind is plugged into a machine
whose matrix thickens
each screen opening onto more screens
and so on and so on.

I wait with patience for the day
when I leap into the arms
of Beauty once and for all
and dream with eiders
in the fog and tide.

—Jenny Gundy, Marshfield

South Florida Sunrise

At 6 a.m. our next-to-last day at Dee-Jays Motel,
we put on jeans, sweatshirts, went out barefoot.
The sky was gray.
Never before had I watched the sun rise on the ocean.
We saw beach chairs stretched out waiting for us
at the edge where the tide was spilling in.
We saw no one.
A few coconut palms waved behind us.
The wind was strong.
Only our foot prints marked the smooth wet sand.
The tide swept up under us and we sat close and waited.
I said, "Maybe we won't see it."
Way out the clouds rested on a gold hairline
suspended over the sea.
"What are those lights out there? A bridge?"
The clouds turned pink.
Far down the beach, two children chased the surf.
When my eyes returned to the white sky,
a huge red head was pushing its way through the horizon.
Turning orange, its full face emerged from the blue water.
Overpowered, the ocean crept beneath the yellow eye.
Earth was spinning.
I felt dizzy.
The birds started.

—N.G. Haiduck, Burlington

How to Greet the Evening Star

If it is January stand in the doorframe
door wide-open to the cold
Look toward the horizon until
blush fully fades   blue deepens
and darkness spreads inky

If it is January return to the kitchen
mince garlic   chop shallots
saute in butter and olive oil
until the smell is like
home all winter warm and amber

Return to the door   now clothed well
Enter the clouds of your own breath
finding Venus just there by the moon
acknowledge the beginning of night
See the first stars as they glow

If it is January remember first times
the way joy first found you
nod in assent and return to
the kitchen to finish making dinner

—*Leigh Gavin Harder, Middlebury*

Kunst Haus Wien (Art House Vienna)

What visions can you realize
By never growing up, by flat-out refusing to comply
With the laws of gravity, perspective, or proportion?

If the Who you were born as finds this impossible,
Change your name! See what it did for Tiny Tim,
Whoopi Goldberg, Engelbert Humperdinck—
The mad fellow who made this place, for instance,
Rejoiced in the moniker of Friedensreich Hundertwasser,

And thereby conceived buildings
That look like Joni Mitchell's ice-cream castles,
Checkerboards who've dropped acid with M.C. Escher,
Or something left over from a Tim Burton nightmare
That real people actually live in.

If you lived in such a place, would it feed your fancy too,
Make you smile every time you came home,
Write books, dash off abstract paintings—
Or would you need to live
As pedestrian a life as possible
To balance out the wondrous oddity
Of your earthly shell?

—*Roberta Harold, Montpelier*

keep it simple

keep it simple
boredom times two
add egg, add water
beat with a spoon
salt to taste
bake forever
throw on snow
they'll find it soon

—Neal Harrington, Warren

All About Hannah

Hannah cries a lot but is fierce
Awesome
Nice
Nature Lover
Amazing
Hannah is good at being Hannah

Thoughtful
Earth Lover
Ammmmm . . . (thinks a lot)
Summer birthday and likes the sun
Everything Lover (well almost)

—Hannah, age 7

Time, You are a Romp in the Backseat, Leaving Me Begging for More

I'm turning tricks for the universe,
begging for one more day,
my heart a stew of lust and learning.
Here, in the very crater of my being,
where I hold my own heart,
where truth flowers beneath the folds of regret.
I am cloaked in a fire that knows boundaries,
yet still tiptoes to the end for one more look.
I do not wait. Well, maybe.
Tiptoeing away from the infection of doubt.
I am a scratched searching, sipping the poison of indecision.
Midlife and sober, I can recognize the stagnant suffocation disguised
    as safety.
No more of this perpetual hiding.
My heart says: Hello . . . Hell no! Goodbye—
My heart says: I'll take a gut-punch of open-endedness,
just be careful not to disappear along the way.
For as long as I can, I will hover in this avid allowing,
in the unbalance of urge and becoming,
in the not yet written plot, awaiting the deliciousness of knowing.
Because requisition of control is as bitter as unrequited love.
And,
Time, you are a romp in the backseat, leaving me begging for more.

—*Tracy Haught, Duxbury*
a different version of this poem was published in *Isele Magazine*, January 2022

Cyclamen

I just wanted to pull her boots off
those spindly arms and hips
and translucent legs aspire

But they're they're seeds not leaves
and I can always fluff a pillow
in a bed full of objects

At least those
apricot ears and parrot lips
bring not transparency

Instead I bought a plant
that quickly turned poisonous
the side affects
red

—Mary E. Hayden, Marshfield

You & I at the Cinema

We race inside from the bitter cold
just in time to buy tickets,
salty popcorn and Junior Mints
before the film begins.
After we settle into our seats
and pull off our burdensome coats,
you lace your fingers through mine.
We always hold on
through the last line of the credits.

These twenty-five years
have not been without loss,
but what has filled our hands
has always been more
than what has slipped through them.
Before the glow of the screen,
I study your profile,
admire its familiarity.
The many lives I've lived with you
here in the safety of the dark
are still ours alone to keep
as we step out once again
into the uncharitable light.

—*Jen Heller, Montpelier*

New Year 2025

Beyond the fence & up beyond the mountain.
Beyond memory, beyond prediction.
Beyond being lost or mistaken
& far beyond the truth.
But also, beyond lies.
Beyond the farthest planets & the fear
    they'll disappear before we discover them,
Beyond the desire to be discovered
But ever prepared for these possibilities.
Beyond reason hearing the hum, seeing the pulse,
Beyond the other universes, breathing the same, connected air,
& yes it changes beyond our atmosphere, but still
Not beyond connection, not beyond belief.

Beyond memory, beyond foresight & forehearing,
Beyond foresmell, foretaste & foretouch,
Beyond forefeeling,
Beyond recognition.

—*Geof Hewitt, Calais*

Maybe Tomorrow

Today I'd planned to write a serious poem.
—It's hard to justify things written for
enjoyment, when there is a greater need
for words inspiring action and debate.
Distilling global issues into art
goes pretty well until fatigue sets in,
then bit by bit my focus on the grave
erodes and something mischievous begins:
My heart, done in by cerebral demands,
inserts a rhythm closer to its own,
a cheerful rhyme and meter take command,
subverting my attempts at thoughts profound.
Before I know it, I am done. Doggone it!
I've lost control and made another sonnet.

—Sam Hewitt, Essex Junction

Lake Winona Basket

A basket is a poem without words.
Earth is a vessel for grief and beauty.
Storm-blue threads tangle late afternoon sky,
spangling the hills, glinting with winter gold.

Earth is a vessel for grief and beauty,
a solemn marsh, deceptively silent
and still. But there, a glint of winter gold
entwines viburnum twigs and low willow.

The solemn marsh may seem silent and still
until your eyes light on the subtle sway
of grass and willow twigs and clinging vines.
Rain strikes the silver surface of the pond

until your eyes see it as an embrace.
Water returns to water, coming home,
the silver pond embracing falling rain,
a vessel for its storm-blue tangled grief.

Rain-softened vines in hand, returning home
among the hills, the sun threatens to shine
before it sets, to embrace tangled grief
and make of Earth a poem without words.

—Cindy Ellen Hill, Middlebury

Blue Eyes

I see your blue eyes
In my blue eyes.
I see them in the ocean,
I see them in the skies.
I see them in the shade
Underneath the maple tree,
My favorite spot to sit in your lap
While you read to me.
I see them in the bath bubbles,
The way they shimmer and they soar.
I see them in the river,
When she lazes, when she roars.
Oh mommy, I see all your love
In your glittery eyes so blue;
And when you look into my eyes,
I hope you see all my love too.

—Angela Hilsman, Montpelier

Snow Stories

It was one of those winters when snow fell by Thanksgiving and stayed

Overnight, tracks appeared in the yard telling stories of fox visits
to sunflower seed feeders where cardinals fly
to feast from hidden spaces in the mock orange

Next morning fox tracks expose paths shared with ermine as white as snow
where both prowl near tiny mice markings well into hunger season.

Goldfinch, downy woodpeckers, and squirrels create lively motion
in daylight hours while fox rests in an unseen den

New snowfall, fresh tracks reveal nightly fox tales of raiding the compost,
travels to the lower meadow of elderberry bushes
and a curious stop by honeybee boxes

Sleepless! I wake at one am and see a figure through the glass door
Low and behold! It's a red fox, with wildly beautiful bushy tail,
strikingly angular face, ears perked up looking right at me,
then without pause, red fox devours more seeds

This encounter with red fox feels of an ancient connection,
messages for me in snow stories, a gift, a winter muse, then snow melts
tracks disappear, red fox moves on to birthing kits in spring

—*Alicia H. Hingston, Danville*

Breath Divided by Three

Inhale
        gathering musty rainy soil
        salty breakfast bacon
        goldfinch's soft landing
        love from a handmade birthday card

Hold
        for the time it takes to
        glance at the passing clouds
        notice a spider on the window
        remember I have breath

Exhale
        beyond the moment of trepidation
        as long as it takes an ode to simmer
        until my belly disappears into an embrace

—Lily Hinrichsen, Bristol
from *The Immensity of Little Things*, self-published

Over and Under

Here over the the lazy Brook
is a roofed wooden span
built strong enough
to not break under weight
and casts a shadow swathe
underneath where trout dwell.
Here under the covered bridge
there is a rocked bottom bed
and a cool darkness against
the harsh heat of day.
Here over the flowing water
is the way home.

—Linda Hogan, Montpelier

Epilogue

The boys run straight for the gap
in the trees & the sun is the whole thing,
wild & whistling high on its blood orange hill.
We're out here throwing frisbees all
uncorked afternoon, cracked open
so the dew gets in & tastes so fresh I
almost forget what it's like to have
fall without the sun, without the cold
dry air. Donny crests the hill & jumps & clicks
his heels like he's unfolding from a page
of a children's book. Behind him
the Worcester Mountains swell fat with joy &
color & Evan follows & they disappear
into the valley, the quiet tumbling onto us like the riotous,
roaring future so bright we can see it from here.

—Matt Hollar, Burlington

Ad Infinitum

Sometimes it happens
When nobody is looking
But it's always there.

—*Stephen J. Holmes, East Montpelier*

April

My microscopic life
looms large
on a day like this
when the white world
pops with the red
of cardinal at the feeder
and I thirst for the full
spectrum of green
due in a month.
When even the dirt roads
are weary, ready to give
up the imbedded frost,
small trickle sounds
breaking the snow silence,
rivulets of thawing
in the woods
and the birds begin
to return, one species
at a time, happy to be
home at last, at last,
spring bounding fresh
against all odds.

—*Sarah Hooker, Marshfield*

Rye, 2023

We comb the beach for stones exhibiting symmetry, mineral homogeneity, sphericality, self-similarity, topologies to promulgate a mythology of embryonic origin: ovoid inclinations, the petrified ova of some long extinct species, impossible eggs of the earth—unhatched and unhatchable—nothing born in their breaking save the very substratum of the world, the physical memory of functionally infinite tumblings.

Nature makes ellipsoid figures while aiming for a future perfect circle or deviating from some supersymmetry in the deep past. And these stones will outlast the body that speaks them into the words used to describe them in real-time or conjure their memory, painting a scene for future hearers. Time is the only transubstantiator.

This Sunday morning, I sit on a bench of granite and think one could do worse for a catafalque or altar. Today, this lovely rock marks a place where offerings are made in the simple form of ritual sunbathing, leisure pursuits, idlings of hours. Perhaps authentic recreation is the highest form of worship.

Lodestone of the petroglyph menagerie, I scour superficial cruciforms into my lithic misericord, symbols of blessing or commemoration, declaring "I was here" in the loaded language of abstract atonement. All symbols are provisional. The water calligrapher, the stone balancer, the maker of sand mandalas: all are right interpreters of the Dao.

—*J. Lucas Hughes, Montpelier*

Chickadee

A thumbnail sketch in black and white,
I dart and dash—with seed I've snatched—
then tuck in tight to hide my take
in nook and niche. A black-capped crook
(though cute as heck), I stash my cache.

—*Mary Elder Jacobsen, North Calais*

The Vermont Dream I Woke Up In

There is a road in my dreams I walk in sunshine again and again.
It runs straight between a white farmhouse and red barns,
by the settlers' cemetery and along stone walls
with a line of old sugar maples and pasture on either side.
Then it ascends into mature hardwoods where the road is thrown-up
but still leads to a clear blue pond known only to the few of us.

One time I climb a nearby mountain with my friends.
But on the way down I somehow lose them and my way,
until I see that sparkling deep azure through the leafy green,
stumble out to the shore, thankfully going for a dip
before heading back, knowing I am on the road.
Listening to a wood thrush as I near the pastures,
startling chipmunks atop the stone wall and contemplating headstones,
I hear the boys at the farmhouse shout and restart their chainsaw.

So walking there with damp hair,
in the road, I came to know
that sense of dreaming in dreaming is a dream.
And that to make this dream something special
is the waking dream.

—CurtB Johnson, Calais

Throwing a Check

"To check": in lacrosse, to use one's stick to impact and manipulate the opponent's arm, hand, and stick in an effort to dislodge and steal the ball.

By the mathematical figuring
of distance and timing,
of throwing your stick out

with one hand, counter
to the cadence of his cradle,
so that your stick swings on

the fulcrum of your right wrist
around the barrier of your
opponent's body and lands

against his own stick
with a sound which, in your mind,
rivals the ring of an orchestra's

triangle in its singular moment,
you knock the small, vital
planet of the ball loose,

sending the opponent's stick
into orbit, spinning and
spinning through the air.

—Daniel Johnson, Winooski

Lola

Lola
Good little doggy
Walking, playing, jumping
Was a loving, nice, cute doggy
Doggy

—Josephine, age 9

what I left behind

my phone/my favorite shirt/my glasses/my last ten bucks/my body/my new haircut on your bathroom floor/my hands and knees on the kitchen floor/my hip print on the mattress/my blanket nest/all those things I thought I wanted/wet ashtray smell/fear of bed head/people who didn't know how to love me/half a sandwich/a full pack of smokes/27 broken hair clips and a scrunchie/my pants/the me who was ashamed/the me who didn't know me/6 pens/one unsharpened pencil with no eraser/a trail of cough drop wrappers (three different kinds)/a confusing mess/a prayer full of noisy tears at the river/my necrotic heart in the Colorado mountains/my perfect latte that fell off the roof of my car/my keys
 /everything that was in the way

—joy, Montpelier

Thanksgiving

Stuffing and Turkey.
Pumpkin pie and cinnamon.
Spice and love.

—*Julia, age 10*

I'm Not

I'm not taking enough probiotics
I'm not getting my recommended daily amount of exercise
I'm not getting 8 hours of sleep a night
I'm not eating 3 square meals a day
I'm not eating 5 servings of fresh fruits and vegetables
I'm not doing daily meditation
I'm not keeping a gratitude journal
I'm not staying away from social media
I'm not close friends with 3 to 5 people
I'm not taking Kundalini yoga
I'm not limiting my caffeine intake
I'm not putting on sunscreen every time I should
But I am living my life

—*Jon Kaplan, Randolph*

Intention

Choose your own adventure: It sounded good
but the handbook didn't separate worst from best,
spell out chances of disaster. Each car rusting, one house
burning down, allies gone off on their own quest.

So it's been a few tough decades of survival,
of making do and figuring out new paths.
Not that it's all been dark—any time the odds turned
there were festive meals, happiness, good laughs.

But if you asked me now what got me through
it wasn't the hours of unending work, or the last
unexpected bonus, the medical payment written off
or anything else with roots in my own past:

Instead, each morning, new light. Each spring,
tender green and daffodils and apple trees
bursting into blossom. The blue skies of summer.
Autumn gold and scarlet that pulled me from my knees

into dance moves that defied the coming winter.
So what if the adventure's not as brave, as bold
as I once expected (no sword or brash reward)?
Walking into each sweet new day—I've found gold.

—Beth Kanell, Waterford

I See My Mother Fly A Kite In Her Backyard Forty Years Ago

turning the white thread in her hands,
pulling and twisting the handle, black hair
flying free in the wind, face raised up
to the clear, blue sky. No sign of sunset
as the afternoon sun beams down. The wind
howls and howls and my mother's dress flaps
without a second thought.

—Seelai Karzai, Rutland

previously published in *Fragmented Futures: Afghanistan 100 Years Later*, Afghan American Artists and Writers Association

Before the Redwing Blackbird Sings

In the spirit of spring, the
maple stretches her branches skyward,
embracing rays of warm, gentle light.
Blue sky, gray earth-
warm afternoons melt away frozen ground,
and brooks lose their cold winter innocence,
releasing a spring torrent of dead winter runoff.

The maple, with her sweet green plumage tucked away,
still rests in her dusky winter slumber until
her roots begin to warm in the suns gentle embrace,
sap burbles up her resting place,
falling in a delicate symphony.

In the distance, steam rises—
sap is gathered, silver and clear,
then boiled thick and amber,
preserved in clear glass jars,
a sweet reminder of spring's first breath.

Spring turns light to sweet perfection.
Crocus' lift their heads in purple and white,
daffodils dance yellow in the still light spring air,
before the redwing blackbirds sing.

—Monda Kelley, Brandon

Melancholy Farewell

Dance with me, sweet Innocence
Hold your defeated head high
Radiate your energy
With beaming, naive eyes.

Dance with me, lost Lovers
Gaze into my darkened soul
Where blurry reflections are fancy, fairy tales
And lurking shadows are perfect widows' veils.

Twirl me towards a false reality
Where days go by with no responsibility
Dip me into murky waters deep
Entangled in my sorrow
With seeping muddy veins, I weep
Of days unable to borrow.

—*Jamie Keough, Northfield*

Your Lips Are Like Soft Paws

Your lips are like soft paws patting my face,
Your paws push my face away.
Your face reflects the warm caress of the sun on my head.
Your head contains the myriad of stars shedding star dust on the ocean.
The seals wave to you like the silkies they are, calling, "Sister."
All is one with you. The whole universe in your eyes.

—David Klein, Montpelier

To my daughter on the cusp of her 18th birthday

You were conceived in the rainforest in a tent cabin
next to a large muddy puddle in which a quiet caiman lived.
The air was oppressively humid and wildly dark.

Love, I've you known since your cells began dividing.
Your compass has always pointed you toward adventure
and longing, and hunger for the next thing.

You cried until you could crawl
and then took off into the world scowling and humorless.
Brimming with questions, suspicious of strangers,
you tumbled through childhood guided by both curiosity and caution.

Child of fierce dichotomy,
you have always craved both comfort and risk, freedom and boundaries,
ease and challenge. Action and quiescence.

Be vigilant for the ennui that lurks in the space between your antonyms.

Be the caiman in the mud puddle in the steamy black rainforest night:
Savage, watchful, staid. Moved only by your own inner voice.

Love, I've known you since my blood coursed through our shared body.
May the magnetic north of your feral curiosity keep you both safe and free.

—*Elizabeth Knapp, East Montpelier*

To Cover the Road

This poem did not erupt wild-eyed
like some escapee from a shell
that fell on moss, shaken from
an oak after a tornado. Or tumble
from a book of fables featuring
women spinning gold with swollen
thumbs and lips fat with gossip.

It curled up on pebbled path,
one wooly bear seeking sun heat
on an overcast fall day when leaves
fell as softly as yesterday, just
more of them all at once

—Tricia Knoll, WIlliston

Sparrow During the Eclipse

I perch on an oak near gathered humans
this raucous herd standing, sitting, standing,
staring at the bluebell sky
light fades without a cloud
I squint, blink, widen eyelids
why does my sight fail?
chill drifts like mist
storm gloom fills the clear horizon
a great shadow covers trees and hills
danger! danger! I hunker down
a massive hawk swoops overhead
snatches the sun and leaves a feathery ring
evidence of the kill

the herd bellows at the sky
ignoring taloned peril
light appears, daffodil surprise
relief trills in my throat
as humans disperse bovine-slow
I fear these clumsy beasts
did their roar chase away the darkness?
or did they coax it here for a hungry purpose?
crows leading wolves to a carcass

—Phineas Knowles, Bristol

It's the Beginning of the End and I'm Here to Tell You

What it feels like to know and to not be believed.
Conspiracy theory, they say. Toss out *crazy,*
overreacting, ignorant
as the other side.
Yes, the side, or site, of my knowing
comes from the woke side (re: empathy),
comes from the heart-side, and the logic side, too
even with no facts or evidence, but what poet
ever gave you evidence of the moon's yearning stare
that was a cold hard fact and not a buried bone
unearthed from their own unknowing body?

I can tell you how alone inside my own skin
I feel for knowing what I know (what I wish I didn't know)
what I see in our future, which was a future my Jewish ancestors
could never know. But I do
because someone with my blood in a German town,
or a Hungarian one, depending on the side (re: how many sides
to a [insert one] family/poem/moon/democracy/aisle/border/body?)
had the sense, or luck, or privilege to flee
so they could whisper down to me,
in, or through, my bones, a voice coming
from the other side of the veil this time
to tell me what the world will become.

—*Samantha Kolber, Montpelier*

Aubade

The floor rattles a day out // whistle incoming // the room comes quick // the dream dusting leftover wings and good glass bottles in the tree leaning over the river // the home is illuminated in the glow // gone left in the woods undone in flame always and again // the dictionary open in place of a bible // crows and foxes coming by to inquire to witness a word returned // the beaten trails an imperfection from the structure // a collapse foretold where cows once grazed // where also a family grafted built and died // nevermind the silo at night // they were lost rooms of other people's lives

two AM breakfast in the corner booth at the corner diner of Portland // friend with a borrowed name catches the neon in her glass to keep herself interested // soothing heat and a plate of grease // the busser beat down the windows to break up the fight // all this town is good for // was it bridges or shimmer // I tell her it's the moss I can't get enough // to the friend simply wanting to recollect here I will give it away // to be fulfilled in a vast ruinous moment chlorine blue walls deep south highway fluorescents tiled matrix // enough for escape

as a sign of gentleness you carried me to the void // the procession // my personal omnipotent thundering // invisible but for the sentinel streetlights puncturing the tongue // I sank behind in the gums expecting shards and frightened teeth to leave me with a path // started suffering // to be so complete and forget the morning has its own terrors

—AP Kramaric, Winooski

Fogies

"Let's make out like them when we're that old."
the teen girl told her boyfriend

when they waltzed by you and me and our PDA on a bench south
of a gazebo on the lawn of the Episcopal church in a village

where we didn't live, when it was dusk.

Her's is homespun naivete: She doesn't know we're not married;
not yet divorced from our spouses.

We're in our mid-forties, which I thought was old at sixteen
too; and she and that boy won't make it

together to forty; but you and I vow
that we'll never stop making out like teenagers.

—Luke Krueger, Manchester Center

Sabrina

Snow from Sato streets
in a cold New England kennel

Soft eyes. Peaceful
amongst the chaos of choosers
louder than chosen

Silent. Waiting to choose

One look. Helicopter
tail selecting Me for eternity

Apart now. No matter.
Both waiting, biding time
until the bridge appears to take us home

Together

—*AB Lafferty, Lyndonville*

An Intent to Commit

I will always walk with you
I'll feel with you
I'll talk with you
Eat a meal with you
I'll cook with you
Sit with you
Read a book with you
Keep fit with you
Take a trip with you
Might nap with you
Hum a tune with you
But not rap with you
Keep the fire with you
Do a sketch of you
Never tire of you
Maybe kvetch with you
I'll sow with you
And reap with you
Lie down in bed
And sleep with you
Wake up with you
Tête-a-tête with you
Remember with you
Forget with you

—*Bernie Lambek, Montpelier*

Queening

The king hides
while the queen
sallies forth to do battle.
The knight gambols
while the bishop works his angles
left to right, or was it right to left?
The pawn steps forward one square at a time
across the battlefield of black and white.
But I wonder if the pawn,
once it reaches its destination
Transforms into the blood-thirsty battler
or quails—a pawn in a queen's clothing.

—*Jannetta Lamourt, West Dover*
previously published in *Wheelsong Poetry Anthology*, Wheelsong Books, 2022

Watching a Deer drown in the Genesee River

if the drowning is remembered,
the river has done its job
made its claim to the spirit

witnessing the bath of death hollows a soul
captures the blackness that can't be removed
songs ring in the basement of a body

to begin suffocated, choking as a trembling parade
the breath turns distinct, honest.
every movement pulls the air out from under

taking balance from steps, poise from grace
the hands of water reach out
the comfort of gentle humanity breaks

—*Christopher Lawless, Jeffersonville*
previously published in *Zig Zag Lit Mag*, May 2024

Perspective

The morning world looks pale as old flannel,
and from here inside appears dead silent.
I'm not sure why this should feel like a gift.
It rouses my inner paganism,
if that's in fact the word I'm looking for.
The stove keeps us warm right through the winter,
even the windows in some small measure,
and so when a flake of snow drifts sidelong
against the glass it dies in the instant.
A pan with ashes to dump in my hand,
I stand unmoving. It feels like a rite.
Outdoors, caught short by the cold, our crab tree
shows fruit that didn't get time to ripen.
I could forge a metaphor if I chose,
memento mori or some kindred thing,
but I balk at that. It feels too easy.
Just past our ridge lies the long wide river.
Under ice, it rolls right on as ever.

—*Sydney Lea, Newbury*

Anniversary

Remember
How it was,
Love?
 When we were
 Two
 And twenty?
Remember
How we danced,
Love?
 When nights were
 Long
 And plenty?
Remember
How we sang,
Love?
 When days went
 On
 Forever?
Remember
How it was
Love.
 And cherish
 It
 With me.

—Maxine Leary, Montpelier

Watching the Enemy Retreat

It's chemical warfare
And I'm watching the enemy retreat.
Its own death postponing mine

I am not a soldier at Flanders Field
Nor an Iraqi warrior dousing Iran.
This battle is on the cellular level

Medical industrial Pac-men
Let loose to feast on my cancerous buffet
Trying to restore my body's balance
To keep these bullish rogues at bay
Forever

—*Michael Levine, Middlesex*

I like...

I like dinosaurs.
Big dino, small dino, fast dino,
Any kind of dino.
A raptor in a tub.
A triceratops in a car.
A t-rex on the roof.
A Microraptor in a pool.
I like dinosaurs.

—*Liam, age 7*

Note to self

inspired by the buttonhole writers

• remember how things were before
we lived five miles from the flood.
• walk more deeply into heart ache
to see what color life is now.

• in the before times
was I shopping for more stuff?
or jamming bouquets down
the barrels of police guns?

• in the before times
was I making more babies?
or marching for the earth
that suffers from too much

of us? how blind I was.
• the question I live is—
is it really too late for hope?
• despair circles like a predator.

• I will wear this grief forever...

—*Cynthia Liepmann, Middlesex*

Coin or Card?

moguls want
parking meter cash
stricken

their credit card revenues to thicken

tho a penny could buy popcorn and a chocolate mint
everyone knows it's now extinct, except
the commissar of the U.S. mint

a nickel's too fickle
to get you out of a pickle
tho one, a bottle's return might earn you

a dime's too slim
to fatten a tip or pay a library fine

lo, the quarter is the coin of power
it'll buy you parking
for part of an hour

it's the people's coin
to be saved from greed's purloin

—*Hugo Liepmann, Middlesex*

Snowshoe Hare

Snowshoe hare,
Hopping up the hill.
Pauses a moment, listens.
Continues into the forest,
Leaving fresh tracks in the snow.
Looking for some fir needles or maybe bark to eat.
There! A branch!
Hop, hop, munch, munch, tug.
Pulling on the branch to get some more bark.
Snowshoe Hare is getting tired,
And finds a comfortable place to rest.
Burrowing in the brambles,
Slowly breathing...
Asleep.

—Linden, age 12

new year

snake says
why do you worry?
so you can't use your arm
so?
I say
but I can't reach
I can't get out of my own way
snake says
I have no arms, don't need them
I just come across what I need
I say
but how do you hug?
how do you embrace another?
snake says
I twist my body, my mind around
what I need
it's enough
how do you stay warm? I ask
snake says
I burrow down deep
seek torpor
slither out into the sunshine
make do with what you have
it's enough

—craig line, Calais

Yiayia Gives Gifts of Meli

Summer

Clear as the Grecian sky

Golden as sun on sand

Glazing my tongue

With the sweetness

of Wild Thyme

Filling my senses

With the bright abundance

of her Love

Winter

Thick as holy incense

As my mother's accent

—LN, Fletcher

Fish

Coral
And so much more of the ocean filled my vision.
I poke my head above
the water
the sound
of young voices laughing,
Waves crashing against the
ocean shore,
fill me.
I drop under water,
relaxed by the cleansing feeling
surrounded by silence.
The ocean was my cleanse,
my relaxation,
my one way to escape the
hectic world
above.

—Louisa, Grade 6

How Light Determines a Day

Just beyond the glass of a bedroom window
determines the way my body responds to a day.
Light beckons the bones, lifts the body out of bed,
loosens the stronghold on the clutch of darkness,
      the mystery of night, when color disappears,
      when the mind takes off in fantasy, to fear the nerves
      and shadows appear to apprehend the senses,
      silhouettes become something new.
When sun and moon are hijacked by clouds,
day is gray, I ache, coffee never tastes great.
Even milk goes sour. I lose my appetite.
Dresser drawers won't open and the wardrobe is drab.
      Though light in another's eyes lightens things.
      Some kind of sun glows from inside.
      Compassion on the street or in halls
      seems to brighten everything.
If the whole world was dark—
city dark, curb and sidewalk dark,
alley and subway dark, walk in the park dark,
I'd find a place to look up and hope to see stars.

—*Jesse LoVasco, East Montpelier*

Distraction

Lord be my distraction
All day and all night
Deliver me deliver me
From this unrighteous plight
Be with me Lord
This day and this hour
Sanctify me with a spiritual shower
Increase Your Beauty within my new skin
Save me Save me
In this world full of sin

—*Brittany Lovejoy, Montgomery*

Optimism

LOVE is a super-power, we use it alot.

PEACE is all around us every single day.

BE KIND to yourself & everyone.

RECYCLE every material you can, because it helps the earth.

MONTPELIER is our community.

—*Luisa, age 8*

"Friend"

You are my "friend"
Only a friend would get worried
About what was in store
But all you see is more, more, more
More hate, more envy, more stealing good friends
Instead of seeing me you just see the end

I always saw you as the person you are
Under my skin you can see the scars
Why do you hide from the person you can be
Instead of growing you just bully me

I'll stand up for me
And I'll stand up for you
And yet all you stand up for is you and girls you think are popular too

—Lydia, age 12

Watercolor

My steps quicken
When I cross the bridge
Near the library.
Today, they stopped altogether.
Upriver, on a wet boulder,
A pale heron turned the
Familiar view into
A watercolor painted by a Zen master.
The bird didn't move, only
The water, drawing and re-drawing
The rock's outline.
Its sound washed the colors of
The stones, the sky, and
The bushes on the banks.
Instead of capturing the bird,
This fading delivered it up.
Its stillness radiated.
While the water and the colors moved,
The heron didn't. I, watching,
Also became still. I, watching,
Was also delivered up.
I could see myself see the bird.

—Michael Madill, West Topsham
previously published on michaelmadill.medium.com, November 2024

Description of a Struggle

How the years take their toll,
forcing us to be Kafkaesque characters
in storied worlds, our lives juxtaposed
against a backdrop of classical music,
simultaneously haunting and soothing,
whose melodies flow like atmospheric
rivers.

—*Kimberly Madura, Essex*

Time

I can't go; I just need more time to be alone and figure things out on my own;
One day just to be be me
I have to hide myself in darkness

Be you in the dark times
You cannot always be strong and happy
You can always be you
No matter what

—Margo, age 10

Flourish

When I left to trace the advance
of springtime down the mountainous coast:
Your parting words were full
of the nutrients I needed
to tend all our plantings
that had grown into memory.
High in the hickory limbs—beyond
my sight—dustings of pollen formed,
suspended on fireworks that burst
against a day-blue sky.
Of course, there was the frosted moon
that rose over a herd of elk. I watched
the heat from their snouts bloom
into light and disappear.
And so, too, we flourish.
Again, then gone.

These days come all too late, my love,
full of flowers that turn so soon. Yet,
they are anything but lonesome.

—Jack Markoski, Montpelier

Grief

Heat lightning stitches zigzags
across night's purple velvet
and the moon beckons
with sequined shimmer, cool
after summer's ceaseless noon.

A fly buzzes its windowpane wings but instead I hear the hum
of machines hemming the edges
of my heart's mantle, jagged
because you are still here,
grief that knows no respite.

I will not rest until each stitch
is buried and this unraveling ends.

—*Lisa Masé, East Montpelier*

Show Up

My eyes open to another day
Will the fog lift? Will it go away?
Sunlight is peaking through the cracks
But all I want is to drift back
Slowly, slowly, sink back under
Back to safety, where I don't have to wonder
If everything will ever be okay,
If I'll ever embrace the promise of new days.
Tune it all out, block the pain,
I don't want to face it all again.
Numbness feels better than salt in a wound
But I fear the loneliness will consume
My every waking thought and hour
Offering no healing or power.
But shadows vanish in the light,
I can't stay in this comfortable night.
I have to make a choice, an attempt to find
A reason to wake, and fight, and climb.
The responsibility is mine,
One choice at a time.
That will be enough.
It's my life, I will show up.

—*Tamara Mathieu, Swanton*

Moon

She whispers in your ear
    Through the window
Frost crawling, frozen jeweled sparkle
    Lace of winter hiding the reflection of
        Night
Those depths
    Waters of nothing
        Ocean of dark sky
She leaps
    Illuminating
A feather of
Light
A memory
Glimmering
    Shining
See her dance?
    She twirls, curls, spirals
        Falling
            Falling
                Falling
You reach out to catch her
    But you blink

She is already gone

—Mayla, age 16

Blessing on the Cow Dreams

Always they tear out of the barn, break through fences,
with only you to corral them panicked, lest they stumble onto Route 100A,
lurch into a hollow, break their slender legs, collide with cars.

The calves bleat for their mother's milk, but the cows have lost all
    semblance of herd.
They scatter, crazed as if in Pamplona; their panicked hoofs striking
    hard on stone.

It's always just you alone, in the woods, in the fields, out by the
    manure pond,
down by the road, waving your arms to gather back the chaos let loose
    in the world.

While others dream of monsters, beasts with claws and fangs,
your terror is the herd's escape, animals bellowing outside the fence.
It's not them you fear; it's you, letting go when you should have held fast,
slacking vigil when you should have stood guard, something vital
    overlooked,
a fence you failed to mend, a gate not shut, a life with gaps too large
for one lone dairyman to ever fix.

I pray, forgive yourself.
When next the dream comes, End the chase. Let the cows roam where
    they will.
Take the milking stool into an empty stall and sit.
Let grace flow sweet as warm milk into your grasping hands
the man at dream's center no longer searching for what is lost.
And who knows—perhaps then they'll come home after all,
saying what has always been true: It was never your fault.

—Katherine H. Maynard, South Burlington

The Sound of War

for Farideh Hassanzadeh

I try to grasp what it's like to live
where war is your neighbor,
the bomb next door.

You wait for its knock
to borrow your last cup of sugar.
Instead, it takes your house
and the child once within you.

I try to trace the etymology of that sound,
where the shrapnel of its consonants unwrap
from around the uncontainable
nucleus of its one deadly syllable.

In the end, there is no word for it,
no word small enough to fit
inside the human mouth.

—Tim Mayo, Brattleboro
previously published in *Avatar Review*, Summer, 2021

Wet Wool Mittens

I can still smell my wet wool mittens
and feel the soggy knit threads from winters long ago

When sisters and I carefully lifted heavy heads
upon the rolled bodies of our giant snowmen

Planting pieces of coal taken from the cellar
into their blank white faces, giving them a view

Of the garden where the carrots were pulled that fall
becoming noses to breathe the clear cold air

As they smiled with mouths made of upturned branches
broken from mother's resting lilac

That would bloom in spring after all the bodies
returned to the earth

—*Elizabeth R. McCarthy, Walden*

Ardor

In their tall glass beaker,
they're burnished
by the copper waves
of sunset tumbling onto glass—
tall tulips, apricot-colored,
alstromeria watermelon-tinged,
the waxed greens with flowers—
minutia really—
tinted like early plums.

It's a freezing March twilight,
just home from work,
trying to thaw out
while staring at the icy lake
and the wintry clouds unraveling
to let loose the very last
rays of dwindling sun—
the breathtaking surprise
of the flowers you just gave me—
their fervent beauty—
elegant foreshadowing of spring,
heating me in the midst of
so much biting cold.

—*Florence McCloud, South Burlington*

Distant Friend
to Robert Young Road in Starksboro, Vermont

The most austere thing in the world is the moon.

There it is, all alone.

A distant friend may keep it company,

Though, like us,

It orbits on its own.

—*JF McGill, Starksboro*

Leap Year Baby

you wanted to return that day
came back hard and fast
your soul flew on the wings of birds
not angels or demons from the past

our universe once set right
by a fourteenth century pope
kings and alchemists agreed
avoid the hangman's rope

poetic license seems to make
four years be extra young:
yet you are a white-haired crone
one who who has always known
the feeling when the birds have flown
and it's time to journey home

—*Maggie McGill, Montpelier*

exegesis

darkness these days is heavy
both real and metaphorical
yet brilliant stars pierce the night
sky with a determination that calms
my despair with fleeting wonder—
some say they sing

the news now is too bleak to read
or listen to so I open the morning
with poetry and in this book
gifted to him on a birthday
he folded the corners of pages
with poems that moved him

I try to parse the lines
to discern what spoke to him
there is no mystery today
his wonder at his daughter
always clear shining
bright as singing stars

—Becky McMeekin, Braintree

All Giving Oaks

You're towering towns with life teeming, some tiny.
Alighting and resting or scrambling for safe
on your arms so far-reaching, angles up to sky pillows,
in your tough trunks, your hollows providing a place
for nesting at night, day sustenance seeking.
Seeds, berries and nuts gleaned day after day.
Come morn . . . Fur and Feather *Withins* became *Outs!*
They peep then they pop, erupting in play.

I watch, breathe, imagine their lives in your care.
You then reach out to me. I calm.
We connect. I breathe in. Set intentions for now.
My mind opens. My worries you balm.

—*Christine Corrigan Mendez, Burlington*

Finding Nemo

poor Pat
had to pay 600 dollars for a new toilet, which
he discovered he needed when he tried to find the
plastic block his son had flushed down there
thinking he was sending the plastic fishes inside
the block to the ocean and freedom.

"Yee hee!" the boy yelled
as the plastic cube lodged
in the plumbing.

when the toilet came out, a water pipe broke,
the seal on the floor needed to be redone,
and something broke in the water tank.

the plumber installed the new toilet, though Pat
might have made out better buying one himself
at Walmart or Home Depot.   and if that kid
hadn't seen "Nemo," none of this
would have happened.

—Bob Messing, Montpelier

Pigeon Perspectives

The bustling city square is filled with cooing
as squads of pigeons squabble in the weeds.
An old man, gently clucking, squats there, strewing
peanuts, breadcrumbs, and some tasty seeds.

A mother pulls her daughter by the hand.
"Those birds are filthy, stay away from there!"
The old man says "You just don't understand—
so let me introduce this pigeon pair.

"Peg and Sam, here, once were racing birds.
Their ancestors were homing pigeons too.
They carried messages—Top Secret words—
through battles, with heroic derring-do."

The man goes on, "They're smart, and squeaky-clean."
"Well, I'm impressed!" says Mom. "We'll watch awhile."
The strutting birds show off and make a scene,
bowing to their partners, square-dance style.

Beguiled, the girl says, "Mama, that one's pretty!
See his neck? It's sparkly purple-green!"
    They'd seen pigeons all around the city,
        but never paused, till now, to see their sheen.

—Christy Mihaly, Calais

previously published in *Imperfect II: Poems about Perspective,* History House Publishers, 2022

You are You

The world is telling you that you don't exist
Aren't real, aren't right
Because you don't fit into the neat and tidy boxes they've made
What utter rubbish
You sit here, in front of me
With tears
Exactly as you are meant to be
Funny, Joyous, Warmhearted
We promise to keep you safe
Protected
Loved
Heard
It's our job.

You just keep on being you

Curious
Thoughtful
Inquisitive
Independent
Kind
Compassionate

You just keep on being you

—*Mom, Middlesex*

Balding Eagle

We're on top of Mount Putney, where three men
are conducting the annual survey, counting hawks
and other migratory birds making their way south.
One man spots what he thinks is likely an eagle
soaring high over the Connecticut River valley,
which, even through our high-end binocs, looks
like little more than a dark dot in the distance.

The Bald Eagle, adopted as the symbol of America's
highest ideals, despite Ben Franklin's earnest protest,
calling the bald eagle, "a bird of bad moral character."
And yet there it was, though barely recognizable,
even to those who sit watch and study such things,
the symbol of all that we strive to be, appearing today
as little more than a far-off dark dot in the distance.

—David Mook, Poultney

Did I Think?

Did I think I was the only person post
2024 election scarfing down chocolate?
A former client tells my therapist friend
she's living on chocolate. Dark. Expensive.
A friend up the hill uses chocolate to
 get out of bed. I plan to expand
my chocolate repertoire from dark
expensive to hot with cream on top.

Post election I avoid retail therapy.
No trips to TJMaxx for me. Well done
Nicky. Then I count: Three books
on mindful eating, one book on stress
reduction and life clarification
(whatever that is) and a set of
overeating cards. (You don't eat
the cards.) A water color book.
A set of watercolor markers. Did
I mention the counter top Ninja Grill
to cook zucchini and broccoli?

Yesterday I bit the head off a
gourmet dark chocolate turkey
and it was good.

—Nicola Morris, Plainfield

Comfort If You're Lost

Take what you're given,
that's what I think.
Make it be enough.

Lost in the hollows,
surrounded
by mountains' dark bulk,
no map or compass:
follow the cold brook
tumbling over stones,
water clear as glass
over the bones
of the earth.
Find your way home.

—B. Morrison, Brattleboro

Candle enlivens
only when lit though it will
dwindle while kindled

—*Kate Mueller, Montpelier*

"The Persistence of Memory"

after Dalí

While time unwinds beside the window,
no boat floats by, not a soul or a saint in overalls,
not even your father, graying and swollen.
There are rules here.

You close a door, lie down.
You sort word from word, spare no one.
The baby who rises from the river turns away,
lured by no more than leaves falling softly to the ground.

She drifts through the mist, lies down
on a mound of soft earth, plump and satisfied.
You are not her.
You stayed caged, learning

the alphabet of abandonment.

—*Giavanna Munafo, White River Junction*
previously published on poetsonadoption.blogspot.com, 2011

for the sheer zest of weeds

the days may still tarry in winter's dearth
and news may come daily of toppling forests, dying fields
extinction and excision from the delicate web of life
it is enough to make one cower behind quilted words
hide heads in shifting sands to block out the burning sun

but look to this firebird in the pavement cracks
leaves like praying hands opening to adventure
fragile petals defying frost and smoke and hard living
green smiles against the dying of our days

a blessing on these weeds
for they know the world does not end today
and they mark the path to tomorrow

a blessing on weeds
the sturdy ephemeralities of this exquisite living earth
for whatever may crumble
there will always be weeds . . .

—*elizabeth murmuring, Barre*
previously published on allpoetry.com, April 2024

Pernil at Christmas

Once a year, I cook a piece of meat
that weighs more than my son
at birth and he was an above average
weighing baby. And every year I think
this is ridiculous. I don't know
how to cook meat. And every year
I am amazed at how I can do this.
That cooking meat
is not an impenetrable code
like something only the Masons know.
And every year the smell of pork,
earthy, herbal, stays in the bath towels
for a few days and I don't mind. We gather
at our table ten people, three generations,
in-laws and first spouse, children
who are still children, daughters
by benefit of a second marriage.
This miracle of the perfectly seasoned
pork shoulder eclipses the erasures
and mistakes, vows we failed to honor,
commitments we did
and still keep, forgiveness
and good intentions as we slouch
forward and we mean it this time.

—Barbara E. Murphy, Burlington

Raising My Spirits

I had no idea how disturbing the election would

Be for me until I had trouble concentrating and was overtaken

By a heavy heart as I moved through my days and on several

Of them heavy gray clouds dominated the sky where I was,

Enhancing my despair, until a day came when the dark gray

Clouds slowly began to disappear as they were overtaken by

A combination of wonderful white fluffy clouds and a blue sky

That glowed in bright sunshine, all of which thankfully raised

My spirits, guiding me to a better place

—*Joan Murray, Worcester*

The Lonely

I'm trying to get good at lonely
Like a card game or a book of complicated crosswords.
Get good at sitting with it, grappling, dissecting,
Turning it over in my hands to examine all its properties.
Trying to learn it like a lesson in an age-old textbook.

But the longer I live with lonely,
The further I'm convinced
That it defies mastery of any kind.
You cannot win it, ignore it, pass it like a test
Or force it into submission.

Lonely just must BE.

It comes in waves or brimming bucketfuls
of confused heartache—And growth.
Perhaps lonely is not, then, a battlefront.
Perhaps, after all is said and done,
It is the lonely that reaches out her hand
And quietly asks
To be held.

—Michan A. Myer, Randolph

Fishing

When children fish
They stand in the stream
Grabbing at sleek sides slipping by

Aging more
Feet planted on shore
Cast fitfully at every flash
Reeling the fish known by name

Old age like fish rot
Head down and thanks a lot
Up on the rocks
Too far from shore
Yet too close to call it catching
The passing fish we're watching

—*J.C. Myers, Calais*

A Holy Thing

A mouth is a holy thing,
Fistful of thickets,
Sponge-tongued,
Cavernous—
Consumes.

A body is a holy thing—
What it chooses,
What is done to it,
What it

Becomes.

Naked strength, power.

Not holy as in Biblical or rite.

As in fever.
As in want.
As in fire.

—Erika Nichols-Frazer, Waitsfield

They Say

They say that by cart and by foot
Cezanne went to Mont St Victorie everyday
then coming back one day
he died for a cold in 1900 . . .
But I sit at the Hospital's Cafeteria daily
and w coffee and sausages at my table
I paint the Spruce Mountain:
Weakening of the modern artist!
I stay away from the mountain
I dont know the smell or taste of it
only the clouding sky.
Some time a friend
tracking on Spruce Mountain
send me some pics.

—*nitya, Barre*

No One Ever Taught Me How To Teach Someone How To Swim

we could walk down to the beach
and run into the water.

it looks warm.
clean, at least.

could always dry ourselves off,
hike back up for the sunset.

yes but no,
no, you're right.

then there'd be sand in our hair.
and our skin would feel like the ocean.

—Grady Nixon, Montpelier

Fable

I used to be a cat
I played with string and slept
Except at night, then I roamed
Locked outside with all the smells and sounds

I am not a cat anymore
Still there are times
When the sun wakes me in bed with its hot fingers
That I am a cat again and satisfied to be

—Penny Nolte, Montpelier

Belonging to November

November's light makes
relentless, restless, scathing demands.
Takes an impromptu departure earlier every day,
no excuses or fond goodbyes, breaks the parting glass.
Days of Grace hiss urgencies through lengthening fangs
to finish, put away, put up, pull up, store, prepare.
Or you could die.
Walking in the last shreds of the day
my body breathes leaf mold,
an ozone tang of snow,
a shroud of woodsmoke
passes over me, into me.
Lighted windows glare out, stark and defiant.
Haggard calligraphies of dead vines and shrubs
scrape around their frames.
Looking up, the sky is a tumult of grey pearl
and I am an ammonite
curling into it,
binding to the smoke.

—Claire Longtin North, Manchester Center

"mother's eternal blanket"

for Joanie

Your love is on every fluttering snowflake
Your wit, ripples in the icy brook
You will be housed in my snow globe
Where we coincide
Generations carried on the wind
The epoch of your devotion
No matter how misguided
Was brought forth,
Not out of wisdom
But of reckless, seething love
As blankets of reality
Hug us for eternity
And silver surrounds you

—*travis alden stargyll nutting, Middlesex*

Too Late

School doors close,
    it is now three.
        The mouse in the hall
            stares back at me,
                squeaking, squeaking, "You'd better flee!"
When I get home
    it's nearly eight.
        The squirrel in the rafters
            calls his mate,
                trilling, trilling, "It's getting late!"
Back at school
    at an early hour.
        The spider in the window
            starts to glower,
                hissing, hissing, "You look sour."
"It's so early
    and I miss my bed."
    The housefly scowls
    as he sticks to thread,
        wheezing, wheezing, "I've been misled."

—Carla (Neary) Occaso, Montpelier

Bilingual (Japanese/English) Winter Haikus

様々なチェロの合奏白鳥舞う
many kinds
cello ensemble
swan dance

四つ足に青きブーツや雪踏めり
blue boots
on four feet
stepping in the snow

ひな祭り小さき幸を愛でる幸
Hina doll festival
happiness to appreciate
small things

待雪草泥んこ顔のままで咲く
snowdrop
blooms
with a muddy face

最後なる雪のごとくに雪をかく
shoveling
as if
the last snow

—*Michiko Oishi, Montpelier (English translations by Rhea Constantino)*

大石道子

Ten-day silent retreat 2024

No

T
 h
  o
   u
    g
     h
      t

W
 o
  r
   t
    h

Saving.

—*Kevin O'Keefe, Brattleboro*

Car Ride Lullaby

Fall back into the night,
the sun is busy elsewhere.

Like a stroll deep in the forest,
footsteps resound ice and snow,
dozing off in deaf hush-ness,
Indulge after fighting softness,
give in to a false sense of ease.

Let me rest for a while,
as if wrapped in down feathers,
the pull of sleep when it's forbidden,
lulled by the wish-wash of wipers.
Someone else is at the wheel,
swerving somewhere near the line
between clock-time
and dreams.

—Ann Onymous, Moscow

Random haikus

All art is enhanced
when I can admire you as
you're admiring it

Luck is bumping your
full wine glass when reaching for
salt—and neither spills

We'll likely get stares
if our frisky upstairs' stories
find their way downstairs

Tea bags, smokes, toothbrush,
an empty bureau drawer:
What remains of her

Ground thoughts percolate,
simmering on the mind's stove
burning, hot, bitter

Priorities shift . . .
when life is strewn, tossed around,
misplaced like lost socks

—*Steve Pappas, Plainfield*

The Animal Wife

Recounts the amount in her head,
getting bigger and bigger as the night approaches.
Creeping like ivy over the pastures.
If you stare up into the sky long enough—
you can pinpoint the moment when the stars are inevitable.
And the oily green meadow grass gives into shadowy
beaten fawn beds beneath your feet. Curled ferns stand
stationary on the edge of the woods, soft and dense.
Laid upon one another like ribbons of reptilian scales.
She knows one day she will return to the undersides
of the rocks, and lie generously dormant beside the snails.
One day she will rediscover the key. And unlock the skin
barely holding back the wild beauty of the evening primrose.
The spotted sandpipers, and washed out buttercups, and gauzy
blue eggshells. She will abandon everything known.
Splitting into the biome like a hurricane finally hitting land.
Like the last crimped red maple leaf swiveling
in the November dusk, ultimately landing on its sleeping brethren.
And fading back into destined, tapered mystery.

—Emma Paris, Putney

Today I Was Aglow, So I Made This Poem

after James Wright

As the red-faced fox darts
Over the shadow-striped snow,
The shore of the lake suddenly gasps, breathless,
And I see that we are all, indeed, made of stars.
Each moment of time is a frozen waterfall.
A tall deer gleams in the coven of pines,
Proclaiming
Your worth does not depend on this.

—Devon Parish, Montpelier

Come Near

McIndoe Falls VT 1973

When Buddhists bought a farm in Barnet
the women in Bev's Hair Salon had stern words
to say about failed Christian Mission Dollars
sent away.
           They'd been invited up for tea…
everyone went.
               "And can you imagine
leaving bare ledge in the living room?"

But when Bev's son brought home
the woman he'd married while stationed
in Thailand   Bev let space bloom
at their family table
               special plates   rare preserves
the younger children clamoring to ask and tell
father grinning at his son
           as if the prodigal had come.
The new wife sat there giggling
youngest child wriggling on her knee
as though they all (including God)
had been set free.

—*Scudder H. Parker, Middlesex*
from *The Poem of the World*, Kelsay Books, 2025

Temperature Rising

There's always a lot of hollering and thundering about
when the sun is out for too long—
when a heatwave is
overdrawn to the point of producing its own sound.
Horns honking signs that
hearts and minds are starting to rise from the sun's fire.

And the foot gets heavy with the screeching of tires.
And the air grows thick with the
weak and the tired seeking relief from allergic tragedies that itch
like bad secrets in broad daylight.

And the eyes search for tears like rain in a fire,
bloodshot and riddled with crossed red lines that speak
to the signs of the times.

—Dani Parkins, Essex

Dreaming of Trees

At field's edge you invite
your elephant trunk with
the perfect eye
one of few large branches that remain
over your hollowed body
(hallowed body)
that beckons

alive with birdsong
(even as you are dying)
into the thicket
the small path leading
to distant possibilities
light filtering
sapling maples
(givers of sweetness)
an architecture of shadows

the golden field rises to greet
rimmed in winter's green collar
feathered fringe of white pine and juniper
a slash of blue pouring down
an endless expanse of invitation

—Annie Perkins, New Haven

January

Snow curls off the roof
 white wave

We shovel until our backs hurt

The cold a hard slap
on our cheeks

The sheep
warm in wool
watch through the fence

February
arrives without fanfare

Light returns

Pots of purple crocus on the kitchen counter

—Melissa Perley, Berlin

my cat lashed her tail
while the ornaments trembled
only one fell down

—Jane Pincus, Roxbury

Ferris Wheel

Up down all around
Seeing everywhere and everyone
New perspectives now

—*Debra Ann Pinsof-DePillis, Montpelier*

tree pose (vrksasana) on Robin's deck

mute the radio
cat
as
trophies
turn up the dirt
drive here the air
is aria~ sun bathes
her windows
moon rolls
sorrow
off the roof
over day
lilies I clap
my eye on the
maple crown
swaying
no
thing
stings

—Verandah Porche, Guilford

On a Mother's Day Hike on Woodbury Mountain

Halfway through the hike, our daughter says,
while shoving through a stand of saplings,
*You should write a poem about
this mountain.* Our girl, Mama, and I
have already rambled past two cascades
and forded two tiny creeks tumbling toward
our lake below. We knelt beside
Dutchmen's britches, painted trilliums,
and wild ginger in bloom. We
snacked sitting upon a dead-and-down
beside the wind chimes of a creek.
When I ask what the poem should be
about, our little girl says, *The mountain or
the wildlife. Maybe a poem about
a bear or deer or flowers.* Yes,
little girl, this poem is to the creek
   that roils and seethes downward,
   the doe who etched her print in mud,
   bears yawning from hibernation,
   ephemerals fading to the root,
   maple leaves breaking from buds,
   and you, little girl, the wildest
   thing your mother and I ever created.

—Sean Prentiss, Woodbury
previously published in *Writing the Land: Channels*, NatureCulture, 2023

Scar

because a scar marks the point of attachment
is it proof

that you do not get over it
or that you do?

the body is proof that you keep going
until you stop

I have never felt broken
just marked up

E said *The only person you can't stop speaking to
no matter how angry you are, is yourself.*

I spent years forming questions
as I sat by the polluted rivers of my city

comforted by the movement of water
which is a language of forgiveness

all force and yielding
the cadence of leaving and being left

—Alison Prine, Burlington
previously published in *Sixth Finch*, Winter 2025

Breakup!

I know you both comforted me day and night

Hated me when I did not match you right!

Days passed by and I really have to say goodbye

My love is not persuaded, it just looks faded!

Let's break up before someone mocks

Oh, my comfy TORN socks!!

—Parvathi Rajaram, Montpelier

Sonnet to Save My Life

It's probable blood stains our sacred lands.
   Fence posts rot, structure's sure, slow reduction
Despite the sweat and work of endless hands
   Sowing and tending harvest's production.

Fires burn hot and bright until they're ash.
   Same too for you, me, and our tiny lives.
The mind's insurrection is hope, a lash
   Wrapping life's rope cut randomly by knives.

We're sad animals who tell our futures,
   Tending psychic wounds with moments of joy
We drag our pasts like unthreaded sutures
   Broken wings are a mother's clever ploy.

Our mouths release black feathers of words.
Our lives ascend in swirls of migrant birds.

—*Kiev Rattee, Manchester*

Song of the Iris

In the long dark
we curl inward
under pale blue quilts;
patient and still.

Waiting
for the light to grow,
for warmth to loosen
the tight wrappings
of winter.

Dreaming of a day
when we will unfurl
and blaze
tender and bright
in the company
of other dreamers

who have also waited
through the long dark
trusting, even in the deepest cold,
that light and warmth

—*Susan Reid, Montpelier*

Snow Is Falling

Snow is falling: Floating, Fat, Fluffy, Flakes
 Looking up, they descend like magic from heaven,
soft and quiet, a new creation sticking to the tip of
      your nose.
Think about it . . . your first step out the door
and you're walking on something
all sparkly, and shiny, and brand new
something no one else has ever trod upon.
It crunches beneath your feet.
Shoveling can wait; the coffee smells good and
the fire is warm.
Your eyes are closed. Your breathing steady.
Looking at you, I find myself smitten—still
                            in love!
Outside, the world seems bright and endurable,
the bleakness of a winter morning is stopped dead in its tracks.
The cold, lonely silence of the new day is welcome and embraced,
even if I'm shoveling snow.
This morning, I embrace you with my heart
                          and wish you a good morning.

—John Reilly, Barre

Memories

Some stick. Some slide.
Some grow fat with sloth. Some lean by running.

Some are mine, some are yours.
Some fuel beauty. Some unearth the grave.

Thirteen years in Montpelier,
Number One on my list of good mooring.

Number Two remains my Baltimore;
I grew up there singing with Orioles.

Between One and Two were twenty-five;
twenty-five different homes where we gave birth to ourselves.

The two of us, we grew into family,
a rainbow of colors, and night.

Some stick. Some slide.
Some stay lean with running. Some grow fat with sloth.

Some yours, some mine.
Some fuel beauty. Some unearth the grave. They have all given birth to now.

—Richard Riley, Montpelier

To Me

To me you will always been a queen
You've earned that crown upon your head
You carry yourself with such sweet aplomb
Goodnight kiss upon your head

To me you will always be an angel
Wings of gold upon your back
You bring joy to all you meet
I'm trying hard to pick up the slack

To me you will always be a goddess
Celestial and divine
Heroine for the ages
I'm so proud to call you mine

—*Greg Robertson, Northfield*

Of Mud and Maple

The Inuit, we're often told
Have many words for snow and cold
Vermonters, then, it's understood
Own dictionaries filled with mud

Or do we? And if not—why not?
Why don't we call it chocolate snot?
Or axle-sucking sink-the-car
Hipsters talking tan terroir

Instead, we sort that springtime staple
Lovely grades of liquid maple
Fancy, amber, rich and strong
Sugar season all year long

When I smell the spring decay
The frost that tries to get away
When our dirt road turns to crap
I'd rather sample maple sap

—Andy Robinson, Plainfield

Fries

I like fries when I
Eat them with salt and
A drink is good too

—Roo, age 8

Cast Iron Winter

We battled the chill,
fall until summer.
Creosote pinched the flue.

The little ones handled
the hatchet, the eldest
mastered the axe.

Steam from the kettle
kept the creaking at bay while
static sparked to the touch.

—*Bruce Jefferson Rose, Monkton*
previously published on allpoetry.com

I don't

Tramp lady enters Bagito's café, hauling a road-worn hiking pack. For some reason, she stops in front of my
table, though she could have picked anyone—maybe she saw me through the window.
Do you have a car? — *I do*, I say
She's beautiful, though you probably wouldn't notice cause you'd have to look past tangled dirty blond
hair, oversized flannel hunting shirt hanging over a frayed skirt reaching down to muddy boots.
Is your car nearby? — I nod yes
Her eyes are clouded with the fugue. I know that look. I've been there, tramping at seventeen down
the Pacific Coast, slogging through rained-out logging towns, planning to kill myself but never quite,
catching rides with people who, just like me, were looking to die though not always knowing,
or transported to a new world by someone who sweetly played a small guitar and could sing
like Joni Mitchell—and knew—exactly.
What I wanted to say was
I'll take you anywhere.   I don't care, Big Sur for instance, Victoria Island BC, cause you remind me how I
always yearn to plummet back into that dystopianized world of liberated self-destruction and abandon
this idiotic ruse that everything's under control, that I am one of those normal people.
But instead I say, *Where're you from?*
Tramp lady frowns and I realize sorrowfully that I've failed her—she'd mistaken me for one of her kind.
But I'm no use, just a dried up husk, part of the real world that doesn't exist if you really—GET IT.
I'm not answering any personal questions, she says
Later, Tramp lady's sitting on the low stone wall next to Doughnut Dude's stand in front of City Hall.
She gives me a quick smile, but might not even remember. I clearly don't matter and I realize it's true
                        I don't

—John Rosenblum, Calais

Four Mountain Postures

Walking in the mountains,
I'm breathing
I'm alive

Standing in the mountains,
sturdy as a pine
it's ok to sway in the wind

Sitting in the mountains
is a way to learn something—
try it and see

Lying in the mountains,
the earth at your back—
what more do you need?

—*Charles Rossiter, Bennington*
previously published in *Big Scream*, no. 60

Benediction

A benediction for one,
for them, for all.

May there be tranquility, stillness,
gentleness, and quietude

that flows like the rivers
that You sing in, bathe in.

May there be solitude, forgiveness,
hope, and respite

hidden under the mossy rock
under which You lay, where You rest so silently.

A blessing for relief
from pain and discomfort

from the earthly realm where you must exist
against all desire, all that keeps you trapped here.

—*Sa Sung Ma, Northfield*

Corner poems

In a quiet little corner,
I sat and wrote a poem,
on a sunny afternoon
in my quiet little home.

I wrote about a lighthouse,
I wrote about the moon,
I wrote til I grew weary
on that sunny afternoon.

I wrote about events, and thoughts,
and places I have seen.
I wrote of grief, I wrote of joy,
and all that's in between.

I feel so very fortunate,
in my quiet little home,
to have a quiet corner
to sit and write a poem.

—*Martha Anderson Sanborn, Vergennes*

Communication

I ran into an old friend yesterday.
An old acquaintance, really.
    (Was my hug too effusive?)
"How are you?" he asks.
"Pretty well," I say.
I do not say:
    I have Parkinson's disease.
    I have trouble hearing, focusing, remembering, thinking.
    I am so afraid of dying.
    Time is so precious, and I waste it.
    I feel dizzy, but I don't go to the Emergency Room
    Because I don't want to know.
    I feel so alone.
I do not even bring out my old stand-by:
    I feel wonderful in this moment because it's so good to see you.

"How are you?" I ask.
"I'm okay," he says.
Who knows what he is not saying.
I hear he has not been well.
Sweet man.
He walks away.
I blow him a kiss.
(Was that inappropriate?)

—Sam Sanders, Montpelier

Queen City Peripheries

Burlington, VT

You are in the cellar of someone else's dream handed a script
which lacks specifics and a deceased director is persistent
about making this flick. Images of Fellini's black and white
beach flashes fast in the foreground.
Back to the black sign of the times here in
Queen City. Two addicts in the building OD'd last
week, one left the scene permanently, but both were
out of luck and stuck because seedy dealers had to pad
the palms of the men who have greed tattooed
on their sleeves. You were an imaginary

witness with severe PTSD and your heart doctor
said to increase the dose so the pressure in your veins
deflates to a cipher state. You try to creep into a deep
sleep but the bed wedded to the wall of the old gun
factory sags flatter with each low rumble
of the Amtrak on its daily run to NYC.

You want to abandon the desire for poetry or peace.
This is all there is in the now of life.
No one's drug induced state can keep them
in an a more effulgent space.

—Susan M. Sanders, Burlington

March Snow

Three days after the Vernal Equinox
thirteen inches of snow fell.
After a largely snowless winter.
Not exactly what we were hoping for.
And yet . . . there is a stark and brutal beauty
 to it all when the sun shines
illuminating a crystalline world.
Cueing us to find reasons to value the unexpected.
Willing our psyches to appreciate the cold
 as we yearn for the warmth to come.
And really, nothing's all that different.
Returning blackbirds converse in the trees
with the same exuberance.
Geese moving across the horizon
call with the same conviction.
The impossible blue of a cloudless sky
is no less perfect and likely even more striking
in a monochrome world.
And so, we dig in . . . and out . . . and wait.
Perhaps something in me relishes the challenge
and triumph of coming through another winter.
Or maybe I'm just rooted, like the trees.

—Nancy Scarcello, Florence

A Conversation Between Friends

Why do you squirm?
And wriggle like a wiggly worm?

>*I squirm to be near you.*

Why do you wail?
Why the constant wagging tail?

>*To show my love is true.*

Why do you stare?
Then try to sneak beneath my chair?

>*To catch a tasty bite.*

Where would you go?
If I never told you "No"?

>*I'd pad along the ancient trail*
>*Greet my sisters, squirm and wail.*
>*Prove my merit, bark and bite.*
>*Then wander home*
>>*And curl up tight*
>>>*And lick your hand*
>>>>*to say "Goodnight!"*

—Carolyn Cory Scoppettone, Middlesex

what is this silence?
self-censoring already --
after just six weeks!

—*Barbara Scotch, Montpelier*

Mountain Stream

I wake up sobbing uncontrollably.
I hug myself trying to ease the pain
It doesn't work.
Wayne, Barry, Knickers, Dennis . . . gone.
It's been months.
I am utterly empty.

The sun shines brightly on a frigid day.
I smile when I feed the chickens. They reward me with eggs.
I work in the yard and walk in the woods.
I move tractor buckets full of firewood to my porch.
I feel joy.
I laugh aloud at characters in a movie.
Friends surround me.
I am alive.

I am a mountain stream cascading over rocks into a pool below.
    Over and over again.

—Rachel Senechal, East Montpelier

Window or Aisle?

Are you vain if you're afraid to fly?

What's the big deal?
Who do you think you are?
Haven't you done all the things?

There could be satisfying peacefulness in knowing this is it.
Something about flying forces you to think it through.

Strange liquid pooling next to the no-smoking sign.
About to drip down.
Is that normal?
Is this it?

Are you afraid to fly or afraid that there's more life to live?
Either way you're going down.

More to resist. More to create. More to care about

Get out there.
Say yes.
But drive.

—Angela Shea, Montpelier

To the Ordinary One

Let the day be yours
Without condition

Allow the warm sun
To have no agenda

You, tender, plain,
Alive to the patterns in leaves
The progress of the buds

Remember yourself whole
Unremarkable as a shell
A home unto yourself

—Michelle A.L. Singer, East Montpelier

Ode to That Picaresque Protagonist Within

I am trying to welcome that star of the plot-driven novel or film or poem
or classic tale found in so many cultures showcasing trailblazers
who take us on rough & tumble, bawdy, rowdy adventures
wild travelogues where they evolve as humans not one whit.
These are easier stories to write and maybe even easier stories to live
and I do so admire ease and adventure, so why am I so attached
so committed to change, growth, development, insurgencies
of self-help and evolution?
There is the writers' table for the complacent. And there is the writers' table
for the chest-pounding athletes of self-amendment. I look for my spot.
Not a stool for the self-satisfied. Not a pew for self-improvement. No.
We know some adventures can only yield exhilaration not progress.
Some epic luminaries change not one iota, and are cherished and welcomed
everywhere and always. I submit, I submit, I submit. I must submit.
I will take a seat at the humble table to sit and sup, sit and toast.
Sit and buckle my swash. Sit and wish only for what I have.

—sb sōwbel, Montpelier

Reveille

Good Morning! I'm the Poppy!
And I am here to purr.
Greetings! I'm the Poppy!
Yes please do stroke my fur.
Let's not bother Uncle Flurry
He's sleeping like a rock
But lucky you! I am the Poppy!
And wide awake at four o'clock.

—*GN Spaulding, Barre*

First Harvest

I was five or six
when I first pulled a carrot
loose from the soil

what wonders grow where
we cannot see—what colors
ignite from the depths

could I carry that
brightness inside? Could I be
a root of wonder

—Katie Spring, Worcester
previously published in Art & Soil on katiespring.substack.com

Summer in Me Heart

Books, gold, champagne, men,
Yellow, gold, crimson red,
A Franklin stove, me big old desk,
Martinis, jewels, all the rest,
I do not mind the gory bits, the looks askance;
Sudden hits and misses; unspeakable losses.
'Cause summer is in me heart and flowers are at me feet,
Your face is in me dreams when I go to sleep.

—Betty St. Laveau, Montpelier

Rocking Heard

Peace is not passive
Peace is a verb
An action
Led by being

In person
Out front and in good faith.
Peace is not passive
Peace is a verb.

Peace is not a performative Tuesday.
Peace is a mandatory realization
Emboldening the right-away
of every which way we need to go.

Peace is not passive
Peace is a verb
Rocking life
And rocking heard.

—Toussaint St. Negritude, Newark

High Holborn Street

Sounding like a river in spring,
the man with aphasia calls the dog
and the dog brings a stick, a bone—
whatever's leftover from yesterday.

His neighbor, the hospice nurse is coming
home from her late-night shift, and rehearsing
the soft thunk the freezer door will make
when she reaches for vodka and glass.

The man with aphasia goes on calling the dog,
conjuring specks of his former life.
The nurse nods at him, wordless.
Early morning is exhausted,
houses empty, the street hushes.
The moon is fading as the sun wedges
into cars and weeds and they want the moon back.

—*Samn Stockwell, Barre*
previously published in *Santa Clara Review*, vol. 110, no. 1

Mooove Towards Justice!

Those in power move like snails across time,
oozing platitudes,
not a poultice for pain.
So slowly they slide towards justice,
treating people like chattel,
not realizing . . .
Snails are so small . . . under hoof.

#BlackLivesMatter
#IndigenousLivesMatter
#NoHumanIsIllegalOnStolenLand
#ClimateChangeIsHERE
#FriendsNotFood
#DisabilityJustice
#WomensRightsAreHumanRights
#AbortionIsHealthCare
#TransRightsAreHumanRights
#RiotsNotDiets
#FatBiasKills
#LoveIsLove

—Ashley Anne Strobridge, Montpelier
from *Do You Believe in Fairies? Compositions of Truth & Nature in Art & Poetry*, Rootstock Publishing, 2025

gifts from my Father

i am Earth, i am Sky, i am
the Winds traveling by across the desert plains
and the rolling fields of grain

i am the fire of the Sun, i am
the light of a million stars
i am the swirling Hurricane, i am
the gentle rain kissing the forest fern
i am the mighty Oak standing resolute and firm, i am
all of these. and all of these are me.

i am every people's breath
releasing their collective sigh
as our bones come to rest
and the eve of our New Dawn is drawing nigh

if you must weep, i pray they be tears of joy
for you and i are forever one, the sum
of all our hearts made whole

the sparkle of my eyes you will see
in the heavens above as the darkness
cradles the Earth, so too i will cradle you
with my love.

—*Karolyn Sudler, Cabot*

Lily

1.
Dog
What do you think?
Do you soar over clouds or battle cat foes?
Do you swim in a river flowing swiftly
or taste scrumptious treats?
Do you run free like a cheetah
or snuggle up with a teddy bear?
What, oh what do you think??

2.
Going outside
Outside! Outside!
We are going outside!
Run like a cheetah pounce like a fox
Roll on the soft grass like a happy baby
Arghh! Now on the leash
Carrot carrots! Chew like a greedy bunny
Inside we go
Snuggle up to sleep like a hibernating bear

—*Ananda Oliva Sullivan, Middlesex*

We live in a world . . .

We live in a world that
wages war on itself,
as we, human beings,
senselessly spread our waste
and burn poison fuels,
melting polar ice caps,
flooding coastal cities,
causing drought, wildfires,
scorching farm and forest,
bringing world-wide famine,
killing fellow species
and our destructive selves

Mother earth will survive,
but humankind will not.

The song of the earth
will be a requiem
for extinct humankind.

Dona nobis pacem.

—Geza Tatrallyay, Barnard

Solstice Moon

By moonlight the Amaryllis grew
Into three beautiful leaves
A flower still forming within

The moon hung heavy
In a maple tree this night
Heavy with anticipation

The clouds sitting low in the sky
could not mask
Her bright

And the moon
Almost audibly moved to the edge
Where the sky meets the mountain

Only to disappear
Surrounding her heart
with a halo
Warding off the most intense
Darkness

—Caroline Tavelli-Abar, Rochester

Once Upon a Time

Tell me what you're thinking
I believe a poem is there
Looking closer you will find
Those stories never shared

Where that sidewalk crack
Has wandered to the road
Rain drops sprouted sprigs
Of tales we need to know

Birds landing on the porch
Each picking a stray seed
Crows pulling at that squirrel
Who wasn't fast enough to heed

Time loosens asphalt shingles
Letting in that evening glow
Peeling paint chips fall away
Showing boards decades old

Now your clock is ticking
As memories reach for words
Fountain pen inks to paper
Affirming you are heard

—*Tobe Tomlinson, Essex*

Rind and Pulp

Sitting in the belly of my love's rusted pickup truck,
salty sea air sighs through the creases of vinyl seats.
His voice hums, curling like smoke against the windows,
softened by salt, by the words only he can hear.

He hands me an orange—its skin scarred,
like the armor my father taught me to wear.
Tough on the outside, but inside,
it bleeds juice—sweetness I thought vanished long ago—
down my wrists, stinging the wounds I forgot to feel.

My love speaks in a language I've only begun to understand,
yet his syllables wrap around my cracks like gauze.
Did I ever believe I deserved to be loved?
Or did I think I was too much—
too broken to be held the way I needed?

But I'm here, here where the sun bleeds through the weeping fig trees,
where sunflowers grow from the cracks,
and I no longer need to wear armor.
His hand rests in mine, sticky with orange juice,
and I believe in breaking cycles—
letting waves crash over us until we're whole again,
until love floods us, drowning us in everything we've always deserved.

—*Evvi Tower-Pierce, East Burke*

The lord is with me and i am trans.

You cannot pray the lord to find me,
For the lord is with me
And i am trans.
I cannot be found
For i was never lost.
I am trans
And the lord is with me,
Wherever i go,
Whoever i am.
I cannot be saved
Because salvation is already with me.
I don't need your fortress, your house, or your refuge,
Because the lord is with me
And i am trans.
You cannot give the lord to me
Nor can you take them from me.
For the lord is already with me, always and forever—outliving your
    ridicule, your disbelief.
You call me many things, but my everlasting name is unknown to you.
You exalt the limitations of your faith with pernicious pride.
Do not be afraid, for the lord is with me
And i am trans.

—*Shawna Trader, East Barre*

Rhyme's End?

I write this in the still of Winter,
You see this in the trill of Spring.
Behind my pen I live in growing fear,
Trapped in your pen your fate is already clear:
Madmen are in power—and all ceases to rhyme.

So I write in a code, One they do not know
And cannot guess.
Henceforth I

Escribo en español, lengua de Mexico,
Tierra de maravillas, de un pueblo magnifico.

No son latinos los criminales
Los maníacos mismos son los abismales,

Solo quiere poder y plata
Y nuestra democracia mata.

But the OED* must have the final word:
From 1384, "to trump" defines the absurd.

—Robert Troester, Montpelier
*Oxford English Dictionary

Socials

The loneliest days were filled with emails and texts
from corporations and businesses
alerts and sounds
no will to hover thumb over
to even like a friend's post
stuck
in a loop
in a year
in a feeling
in a song
in a memory
or in dings
notifications
from heartbeats
that have slowed down.

—*Gina Tron, Barre*

Shorn

we got in the tractor to pick up fence pieces
to divide the sheep tomorrow.

Shearing Day, of course the coldest day in April,
but they will be relieved of itch and wool and hay pieces and last year.

the person coming, a master of judo, locking holds and snaking limbs
barbering is secondary.

I walk next to the tractor as you back it down the driveway and can see
    my breath, can see the sunset and the purply pink clouds floating
    in sherbet sky.

I'm faster at walking than the tractor goes with pallets and metal
    pieces stacked in its jaws.
my thighs chill inside my jeans but the gloves warm my hands to the
    point of sweat,

and we lift and carry and set up fences inside the barn.
sheep do running laps, stopping on a dime just short of where you
    stand tugging on a ratchet strap,
Sally and Fancy and 1736 coming for requisite scritches while the
    yearlings look on from a distance
then take off in full sprint when I step in their direction.

tomorrow, the wool clumps will be clouds freed from bodies,
    reflections of the now-bruise-purple
ones in the sky.

—Tamsen Turner, Albany

Renaistre

I stagger squinting,
stunned and grateful,
wanting and weak
into the dusty Easter morning light,
my skin almost translucent,
my heart as well.

The winter was long.
I was so rarely out of bed.
How was it I got through?

Oh, yes, you . . .

every day someone showing up,
the sound of boots on my porch
someone loving me enough to walk my dog,
shovel the path,
send beauty and strength,
bring water and food,

leave words

Trust, Believe, Stay

scrawled on little scraps of paper
under the mat.

—Betsy Unger, Montpelier

The Visitor

She appeared in the northern sky
shimmering in the night
a mute mystery drifting high
above the snow so white

Beneath her gossamer cloak
a red gown slipped in and out of sight
billowing in wave on wave
on this cold and windless night.

Bewitched by brilliance of dancing ribbons
of soundless shifting light
I watched this ballerina drift back
into the dark mysterious night.

—Nancy Vandenburgh, Milton

Today I Was Extra Sparkly, So I Made this Poem

after James Wright's poem "Today I Was Happy, So I Made This Poem"

As the golden coyote prowls and howls
Across the cornfield by the frozen creek,
The pinky sunrise clouds suddenly open eyes wide,
And I see that we are all sacred.
Each moment of time is in an uneven plateau.
A heathered hawk pierces the Mystic mother's desert
Crying
I am electric, alive in my element.

—*Emily Walker, Middlesex*

written with Devon Parish at Blossom Wellness during Poetry & Poses

Empathy's Crown

Where do we authorize the sheep for their new brains?
They can skip and climb this murmurous US Terrain
But don't understand the risks.
Why can't they read the fine print
At the bottom of these cliffs?
See the tattered flag? The empty
Husks of once-held trusts?
And where can we find a border collie to
Herd them east, and down to the
Green valley below
Where Empathy holds her crown?

—Kim Ward, Montpelier

Journeying

As my journey continues
I am with wind

I **am** wind
The gentle breeze
The stormy storms
I grow wings
Taking me to watery places
Wind and water touching as friends
Water touching my hot body
So much heat
So much inner fire
Water cooling and soothing
My cells and my soul
A gentle, cooling, heavenly touch
Arrives and caresses
The scars burnt
Into my body and soul
I am leaning into the touch
Welcoming it so
And know
There is always love
I can find it
 and it can find me.

—*Ulrike Wasmus, Calais*

Piano Man

The whisper of the wind
through the leaves is
awakened by the first
chords of a nearby piano.

A brief break allows
the source to be located
before the tunes quickly
come back to life.

A hummingbird adds a
calming sound while crows
voice their displeasure as
fisherman set up to fish.

The tunes usher in
the night as the wind
dissipates with the light.
The piano man plays on.

—Roger Watters, *Shelburne*

Parking Lot Philosophy

Oh my, what if I told you
what I saw on a truck's back window
at the shopping mall today?

Words that first made me
just burst out and cackle,
mirthfully holding my sides.

Then, actually, staring, never having seen
such a phrase, such an admission before.
Then towering over me—my thoughts,
my fears, my anxieties of our time.

the Greek tragedian, Aeschylus,
wrote of the importance
"to tame savageness of man
and make gentle
the life of this world."

What, you ask, was on the back
of that parked truck?
"Please forgive me.
I was raised by wolves."

—Janet Watton, Randolph Center

May Third

has space around it, unafraid
with strong legs
and purple sunglasses.
The car windows
bring in real
breathable air. The kind of open
that doesn't mean danger
or pain. The sounds
that come are not
signals of distress. There's
a bird, a
call
of imminent pleasure.
My Mammy
done told me it's ok but
wiggly in paradise. Paradise has to be chipped away at
to feed
its ongoing
need. There's a place
for you, she said, looking up
from the bottom of the stairs. Her voice
a song that carried
a path
to the song.

—Sharon Webster, Burlington

Socks

Putting on your socks
one at a time
ever so careful
feeling the thin of wear
and days gone by

Your socks are
a colorful departure
from my blacks and whites
each one a reminder
of your footsteps
our shared paths
cozy toes

No explanation can
Stop the fray and holes
No needle and threads enough
To keep the past intact
Or keep you alive

—T.Wendelken, Montpelier

An Untitled Piece

Loneliness and Despair crept inside
To get out of the howling winds and shrieking rains
Of my battering soul-speak.
They crept into my heart last night, and kicking out Apathy
Made love on his bed. The house that is my body felt this
And I tore at my arms and wrists
Viciously trying to expel the intruding lovers. Apathy
Being misplaced, displaced
Got angry. And threw a fit on the lawn of my small intestine.
I tried to soothe him. Giving into the pains of chocolates
And sweet fruit.

—Zoe Whalen, Montpelier

A Pa's Thanksgiving

The morning after it's up and down between cereal bowl and window—
    up and down
faces pressed to the glass, close as possible to the feeder—cardinal,
    nuthatch, chick-a-dee.
"Chick-a-dee-dee-dee," says one, "Chick-a-dee-dee-dee, chick-a-dee-dee."
And all join in—again and again and again and again— the morning's
    blessing.

I spend early mornings with these three—
books and puzzles and winding, branching conversations—
cuddles and laughter, rough housing and train tracks circling through
    the house.
And then outside, coats over pajamas—identifying tracks and making
    snow angels.
Thanksgiving is neither pie nor parades on the television for me,
but these wood stoved winter dawns—their parents still asleep —
where we come to "know one another in that which," as the sage said,
    "is eternal."

And then they leave. Of course they leave. It's preordained, I suppose,
    these departures.
Amid last trips to the bathroom, hugs, kisses—a time honored horn toot—
    they are gone.

Train tracks taken up, toys in the box, books again on shelves—
sheets on the drying rack, a run of the vacuum, a quick floor mop—
and soon the house seems in order, and quiet. An empty kind of quiet.

The next day, alone with my coffee the birds arrive—cardinal. nuthatch,
    chick-a-dee.
The window, I see, escaped my cleaning—Grateful for echoes of
    yesterday's presence
I'll leave the fingerprints and the nose smudges. Chick-a-dee-dee-dee,
    chick-a-dee-dee-dee.

—CD Williams, Williston

Wolf Moon

When the moon is full
And tilts casually against my window,
The way that light-haired attendant
Leans on my car
At the Chevron station down the road,

I flip my pillow to the cool side
And dance cheek-to-cheek
With dreams of tall tick-free grasses
And the rock in my shoe that felt like a friend.

—Emily A. Wills, Fairfax

Change The Channel

I turned on cable news today but couldn't tune out the Beltway.
I scrolled on my FYP but was left deaf, blind, unfree.
I signed up for Luma to make a friend but couldn't stop the feelings of pretend.
What is wrong with how I see our society?

Is it only me? Or is it we? I wish to be free. This is my plea.
We must change the channel in how we portray the world today.
Switch the color spectrum to bright rainbow hues, not reds and blues.
Speak kindness into existence, not using AI assistance.
Listen assiduously, no clever once-over snickersnee.
See through the static, with chromatic, past the dogmatic, and stigmatic.

News only informs when others plan and a revolution forms . . .
But now we observe either Lotus Eaters or reaction swarms.
Both lead us to the abomination of desolation.
No eyes, no ears remain—only wicked words and tears in vain.

So, update your algorithm, break out of this prison system.
Thicken the slurry of sludge content, look up and reorient.
Ignorance may be bliss, but in the end, it is hit-or-miss.
Confidence soon sours to pride; don't let hate turn you inside.
Scan the airwaves for some frequency that musters courage in you and me.
For it's easy to be careworn before the calling of Gabriel's horn.

—M. Wilson, Barre

Someplace That Will Make the Soul Less Thirsty*

Nobody knows the name
you call yourself at dawn nor
the one you go by at midnight.

You stride along under the sky.
At each moment of the sun's
turnings, you murmur to yourself,

give yourself a new name
for each dark to light, today
to tomorrow. You don't go off
somewhere else, you are not

a traveler. You pace *this* ground
near *this* riverbank, stand in
this house full of memories and
thousands of your discarded names.

—*Heather Wishik, Woodstock*

*The title is a line from Kabir's poem "I Said to the Wanting Creature," translated by Robert Bly.

Thrush Solace

I sit in comfort beside my little stove
watching the raging wind bending boughs
hoping this late April gale is at last bringing spring
and is not just a gushing front that means nothing
I am glad I have travelled and have seen
places in our world where ocean tempest seethe
It has given me perspective to more appreciate Vermont
though it is a place where only the patient get what they want
Out through my square of glass the grass is green
Maple trees are budding but are still winter lean
I hear that the ice is out on all the lakes and ponds
which perhaps explains the recent return of our bird songs
It's a wonder brave Robins can bear today's whipping chill
This gusty day our birds are concealed, their songs still
I suspect the Thrush's solace is confidence
Sure that chicks will grow with springs eventual abundance

—Carl Wrighton, Hyde Park
previously published in the *The River Arts Poetry Review*, River Arts Morrisville

Buttons

On the really grey days, sometimes
I entirely forget buttons exist.

I imagine trying to wrap wool
around frail shoulders and think:

there is no possible path to closure.
How do we expect to hold things together?

There will be pulling, heavy, try as we might
and nothing

on the other side. Then, I remember:
the spare on the garment's underside.

—*Bianca Amira Zanella, Rutland*

This Ash Tree

You were once there, and now, so am I.

In this ash tree, with its white burnt bark,
its long branches stretch
as if they're eagerly reaching for the sun,
a gleaming, hopeful jewel.

This tree is getting old.
One of its branches falls.
I wait for a depressing thump,
but there is only silence.

Dark, gray silence,
like bent nails on a dull chalkboard
and bright flashing lightning piercing the silent night sky.

I climb down the tree and stare up as high as I can.
The tree refuses to collapse and holds its head high.

I know someday another child will climb this tree, where I was.
They will follow my footsteps through the light, delicate snow,
over the hills, and back again.

—*Zora, age 9*

Electrical Hazard

Dear rubbery fingers, I've twiddled
the dishes & scrubbed
the rest of the mission entirely. Back
to the cutting board.

I was born bored. I yelped & yawned.
Day after day dawned & sank. I hid
my agenda deep in the dumpster chute
where a snagged patchwork catnip
toy dangled & sprang.

I keep the right hand
in the right glove. It remembers
depressing a lever to lower slice
and slice in the toaster slots. The left
hand wrangles its own
glove inside-out & itself therein
over & rightside out again.

All comes to an end. Surely
something we did might sparkle! I do
remember liking morning love
best when it sizzled & stuck out its tongue.

—Martha Zweig, Hardwick
previously published in *Matter: A Journal of Political Poetry and Commentary*, May 2021

SCHOOLS

Calais Elementary School: Samantha Jackson's Third and Fourth Grade Class

All I Have All I Have All I Want

All I have is chirping birds & beautiful cherry blossoms
The waxwing flutters through the trees

Watch the flowers with the bees
The morning opens up on me

beautiful scents go through the air
A cooling breeze goes through my hair

Grab my tea and sit down and let the world swarm around.

—Caleb, Grade 4

Leaf

Leaf is light
Leaf is very bright
Leaf is quite nice
If you look at it twice
It will look like a dice
Which is double nice in my advice.

—Clara, Grade 3

Calm

Calm is like the color teal
Calm is like a flower that blooms
Calm is like a sweet treat like candy and ice cream
Calm is like you and me also everyone no one is not calm
Calm is as sweet as anyone can be you be you don't let anyone say otherwise.

—Emma, Grade 4

Penguin

Penguins are endangered
Everyone should know that
No one knows why
Go to Antarctica & you will see 7 types
Would you like a trip to see them?
In the winter you can not see the sun
No one knows why!

—Fern, Grade 3

Winter

Snowy
Cold
White
Icey
Drippy
Slushy
Tiring
Below 0
Drying
Can be annoying

—Finn, Grade 4

Crow

I was walking in the snow
When I saw a crow
It was funny you know

Because the crow was as white as snow
So I picked up a ball of snow
And threw it at that crow
You know

But that crow had other plans
so
Right back at me he threw some cans
So now you know how my day went
And I think I need a fan

—Hazel, Grade 3

That Chicken

I went to see my chicken.
But instead I got a licken from the chicken.
I wish it wasn't my chicken.
I wish I had not got that chicken.
Because I got a licken.
Oh, I do not like that chicken.
Because it ate my mitten.

—Hazel, Grade 4

Soccer

Fun, when you want to run you can run.
It is very exciting when you score a goal.
It is very interesting
Soccer balls
and
making
goals
because it's fun
I love to play
And that's me.
But I'm just telling you
It is fun to play
And you
should
try
It
.

—Henry, Grade 3

Soccer!

Soccer, a team play
Goals, gets your blood going
Balls, fun to play with
Shooting, a key skill
Dribbling, important to get past defenders
Passing, give people a chance to have the ball
Defending, not letting people score a goal
Forward, up front in the action
Mid field, stay with the ball
Subs, new players new opportunities
Exercise, running all game or practice
Running fast, power yourself through anything the game throws at you
Goalie, the one to stop a goal
Grass, a plant
Net where the ball goas
Cleats pointy spikes on the bottom of sneakers

—Jase, Grade 4

Trees

Trees.
We think that trees just grow and make leaves
but NO trees talk through the wind,
they listen through the branches.
So don't underestimate them
because they are always listening.

—Liam, Grade 4

Stanley

Stupendous
Thirsty
Amazing
Neat
Liquid
Elegant
Yellow

—Lillian, Grade 4

Gloves

I want to go
Play with some snow
Outside where I find
All my toes.

I went outside to play
with some snow
And I didn't have any
gloves so can you
Give me some now?

I wanted to play but
Then the wind blew it away
so inside
I had to stay.

—Livy, Grade 4

Red Gems

Red gems walk and talk
Red gems talk and walk
But do red gems walk and talk and talk and walk
Nobody knows because red gems can't walk or talk

—Maggie, Grade 4

Pond of Fish

There was a pond
It had no lawn
There was a bob
Inside The pond
It was in Vermont
Inside the pondy
With a Monty

—Monty, Grade 3

The Tree

as the petals swirl
the tree bends and sways in the
wind swishy swashy

—Odessa, Grade 4

Dog Man

Comic
Funny
Dog cop
"Smart"
For any body can read it
Any season
At school
COPS

—*Oliver, Grade 3*

Hockey

Fun
Hard
Ice
Snow
NHL
Stick
Puck
Slap Shot
Goalie
Goalie Net
CANADIANS
RED, WHITE, BLUE
Team Sport
Penalty
Penalty Box
Penalty Shot
Pads, Skates, Teams, Serious!

—*Owen, Grade 3*

Football is a Good Sport

Fun
Tiring
Exercise
Cool
Ball
Padding
Jersey
Helmet
Tackling
Running
Throwing
Catching
Gloves
Cleats
Touchdown
Water

—Parker, Grade 3

Petunia

Petunias are like little fallen stars
small and pretty
Petunias look very tasty
but don't eat them,
they are toxic!

—Ruthie, Grade 3

Dirt Biking

Dirt biking is fun
Dirt biking is hard
Dirt biking is stressful
Dirt biking is awesome
Dirt biking is fast
Dirt biking is dangerous

—Ryan, Grade 4

Rain

Rolling rain pours down from the sky,
All the rivers lakes and streams begin to overflow,
In the distance flashes lightning bright as the sun,
Never ending rain like the drumming of drums

—Sam, Grade 4

Earth and Its Beauty

If you really look,
Everything is beautiful
Just open your heart

—Shepherd, Grade 4

Main Street Middle School, Montpelier:
Kiki Adams's Fifth Grade Class

Together

Found poetry inspired by the words of Dr. Martin Luther King Jr.'s
"I Have a Dream" speech

Sit down together
In a nation where freedom
Rings from the prodigious hill tops of new
Hampshire to the snow capped rockies of colorado
Everything deeply rooted in the american slope that seems
To never end.
together we can climb that slope and
Overcome whatever lies ahead but still we must
Hold hands together!
Sit down together!
Dance together!
free at last

—Alastair, Grade 5

The Moon & Sun

The Moon is hidden through all these black obscurities,
It has many sides, or rather phases; which are all true
Each phase is different, but in the end,
but It's still the Moon
The stars are its moral companions through the ever lasting night
Each star eventually dying off
it's aura is dim, but some see it as the Sun itself

The Sun is shining through all these white obscurities,
It has so much energy in one personality, only one...
Every side of the Sun seems the same but some sides are glowing
with anger, the frustration unreal,
But it's still the Sun
The clouds are its ever-moving companions traveling all over the
Earth,never staying in one place..
Each cloud changing every moment,
Its aura is so bright, but some cant see it at all

Both sun and moon in different worlds

—Alekhya, Grade 5

Things I know

I know we all used to fall asleep in the car right before we got home
so our parents could carry us inside

I know we all did like 12 push ups then go to sleep and wake up
thinking we are super strong

I know we all tried to sneak into our parents room right before a
holiday to see what they got us

I know we all remember when school was actually fun and not hard

—Charlie, Grade 5

Five senses poem

Life is nice and brown.
It is small.
smells weird.
Sounds calm and peaceful.
It feels calm.
It tastes weird.
Life makes me happy.

—Cylas, Grade 5

Mixed

Peru
Hot,colorful
Swimming,calming,relaxing
I switch to Spanish to English so fast
Snowing,Depressing,Glisting
Cold,gray
Vermont
When I'm still in Vermont all of Peru still comes to me.
I'm a girl who's colorful in a place that is not.

—Erica, Grade 5

Soccer

Soccer is fun
It looks like green grass.
It smells like fresh air.
It sounds like "I got ball."
It feels like warmth and happiness.
It tastes like fresh mint.

—Hannah, Grade 5

Death master of life
He will take everything away
Only your body will stay

—Jacob, Grade 5

Patches

(My cat)
my
Patches is coal black.
She looks like the night sky speckled with stars.
She smells like a burnt meal yet it is perfect.
She feels like the moon's light shining on every living creature.
She sounds like the harmony of many different singe
She tastes like licorice, liked by some and disliked by others.

—James, Grade 5

Cool Poem

I just ate my cat
But I got hit by a bat
Now I am a rat

—Jasper, Grade 5

Waves

Waves of the deep sea
Waves of sound of air of movement
Waves of silence of music
Waves are everywhere

—Maia, Grade 5

Moving

Moving, it's the worst
It sort-of makes you want to burst
From the friends who were with you all the time
To nature's perfect little chime
Losing all these things
Even the little bird that sings
I will always miss it there
Having to leave it all, I wouldn't dare
But it's done

—Miles, Grade 5

Japan

Japan is fun and Gold
It looks like huge malls and lots of shops
It smells like sweetness
It sounds like friends and family
It feels like fun
It tastes like yummy foods
Japan makes me feel happy

—Nami, Grade 5

The sun and the moon

Sun
bright,light
shining, blinding, warming
Big star Giant rock
lighting,chilling,looking
Cold,dark
Moon

—Nate, Grade 5

I am

I have two coily horns
I'm a stubby little thing
I'm white as snow

—Rex, Grade 5

Liverpool is cooking up
hopefully they win the cup

Manchester city sucks
they are like sitting ducks

—River, Grade 5

I Play

I play well.
I play hard.
I play nice.
I play competitively.
I play alone.
I play . . .

—Roddy, Grade 5

Strawberries

Red, Juicy
Picking, Eating Preserving
Pretty fruit, Ponty veggie
Peeling, Steaming, Roasting
Orange, Crunchy
Carrots

—Rosa, Grade 5

Here

Here is where I put on my soccer cleats for the first time
Here is where I kick my ballet shoe at the mirror for the first time
Here is where I learn to tap the keys on the piano the right way
Here is where I get my first puppy cute and cuddly
Here is where I laugh with my best friends
Here is where I am right now, breathing, liveing,
HERE

—Rosie, Grade 5

Things I Know

I know how to walk, talk, and breathe.
I know how to kick a soccer ball.
I know how hard middle school is.
I know my friends will love me no matter what.
I know how to draw well.
I know adults get scared even when they say they don't.
I know about politics.
I know the world isn't fair.
I know my family, and how much they love me, and they know how much I love them
I know being proud of who you are is important.

—Simone, Grade 5

Chill goes down my spine
As I step in a tundra
Filled with snow and ice

—Tess, Grade 5

Things I Enjoy

I enjoy playing with my animals
I enjoy hanging out with my friends
I enjoy riding my ponies and horses at sunset
I enjoy time with my family
I enjoy making music and performing it
I enjoy being in theater productions in Hardwick with my mama I
I enjoy playing board games with my papa
I enjoy reading on a rainy day
I enjoy meeting new people
I enjoy making a painting on an empty canvas
I enjoy traveling to places I have never been with my family
I enjoy seeing my cousins, grandma, aunt and uncle and there puppies in Brookline
I enjoy every Christmas going to my nana's house and setting up model horses together
I enjoy baking something sweet in the kitchen
I enjoy sleepovers with my BFF's
I enjoy noon creemees in the summer with my fun mom
I enjoy hobby horsing across the street from my house in a parking lot
I enjoy my cozy little life in Vermont

—Tillie, Grade 5

Main Street Middle School, Montpelier:
Debbie Goodwin's Sixth Grade Class

Space

Feeling really weird
Slowly floating and flying
Why am I in space?

Glimmering bright stars
 Fire looks me in the eye
Comets fly by me

Lifeless dim planets
Sends cold shivers down my spine
I hover calmly

—Adler, Grade 6

In the Forest

The pine trees stand old and tall
Among the saplings young and small
The forest floor is covered in needles
Home to spiders worms and beetles
The sun is shining all around
Casting shadows on the ground
A fox trots past the evergreens
While all the critters are unseen
The bluebirds sing a cheery song
While squirrels and rabbits hop along
 Aromatic scents fills the woody air
 Tiny chipmunks scatter elsewhere
The elegant sunset a beautiful crimson sight
Followed by twinkling star speckled nights
In the morning the soft dewy light
The fresh warm breeze, the day is bright

—Alvida, Grade 6

Basketball

The basketball is as small as a baby fish.
thump thump when it gets bounced
throwing the ball up for tipoff.
Basketball players' jump for the ball *swish*
rubber smell releasing from the basketball
sweat on the basketball players
basketballs swish through the net.
Players' parents are happy when they make a basket and get mad when they foul out.
Coaches are really excited when they win and mad when they lose.
yelling from the crowd. Sometimes it is joyful, sometimes it is not
 because they are angry,
but most of the time it's disappointment because they are mad that
 they lost.
Blowing the whistle when someone fouls or travels. Time table, foul,
 foul shot.
Passing the ball, telling them how many more foul shots they have left.
I am the referee.

—Audrey, Grade 6

Stars

Gaze up at the stars
What do you see? Hear? Wonder?
Stars shine in the dark

Hear the distant roar
Of a train in the distance
Now what can you feel?

Warm air on my skin
Hidden wildness within
Begging to break free

—Beatrice, Grade 6

Dark Sky

I saw the crimson dark sky.
There was not a hint of gleam,
hard rock was going to fly
my red ears would roar and scream.
But I fought the storm,
it was hard and rough,
I defeated it.
Then I sat down and lay
where I saw the clear warm sky;
the yellow sun brighter than ever,
and all the animals were now in safe peace

—Camilo, Grade 6

Seasons

Fall
The crisp orange leaves
The bare brown limbs
The start of long sleeves
The blue sky dims
Winter
The bright white glaze
The wish of the beach
The silky smooth roadways
The spring within your reach
Spring
The leaves return
The birds start singing
The middle of the season
The summer's ringing
Summer
The blazing hot sun
The glowing water
The moons spun
The air gets warmer

—Charlotte, Grade 6

Unwind

In the buildings, with the people,
swarming in their crowds.
All are talking, all are shouting,
everything's too loud.
Social rules, like secret codes.
I do not comprehend,
What's ok to ask and say?
Hard to make new friends.
Then I look, see a door.
Leading to outside,
left the building, left the people,
can't manage, though I tried.
See the forest, keep on walking,
need to get away.
From the rules, from the crowds,
from not knowing what to say.
In the forest, see green treetops,
dancing in the wind.
See the birds, gripping branches,
feel my mouth start to grin.
Keep on walking, see a river,
swirling fast and deep.
Dip my hand in, feel a current,
Still hearing the birds cheep.
Walking on, see a clearing,
lit up from the sky.
Sitting down and smiling big,
so joyful I could cry.
The trees, the birds, the river deep.
Bring me peace of mind,
I don't want the crowds of people
I just need to unwind.

—Connor, Grade 6

Pizza

Dominos is a pizza feature
Their tasty toppings are cool
I think their perfect pizza
Should be served in school

Positive pie tastes amazing,
Their broccoli-garlic toppings are delicious,
Warm pizza is so good, I think, while I sit here quietly awaiting
Their pizza is better than money, it's not fictitious

Penzo's is awesome
Their small pizzas are satisfying
Their pizza's saucy taste is flavorsome
The feeling of biting into their pizza is gratifying

—Dex, Grade 6

stay safe my melody

Wind blows
like a wave in the sky
looks so mellow
but fast and furious, so high.
People go inside
gather their families
we have to decide.
The wind is blowing like a melody
or a rhyme
so powerful,
so fierce like a crime.
The sky is gray and the wind will pull
tiny specs of light falling from the gray sky.
It looks so beautiful just don't go outside.
Don't put anything out there or it might fly
far, far away like a leaf on a windy day keep your family inside.
Stay safe be careful, you don't know what's going to happen
there could be rain or snow just stay safe, even though you're fearful
Stay safe, my melody, this is a lot of action,
stay safe, my melody, you have a long way to go.
Stay safe, my melody, this is a hard fight to win,
stay safe, my melody, the wind is getting low.
Stay safe, my melody, stay inside the wind will spin,
Stay safe, my melody, stay safe.

—Donnavie, Grade 6

country over city

Lights blare and blind me,
cars speeding all around me,
People everywhere.
Ambulances wailing,
men yelling while drinking lots,
Trains rumbling down tracks.
Shaking houses near,
smoking that gives health problems
and disgusts people near.
People running through the
streets with horrified looks on
their faces. Running.
The city is not my place.
Chopping wood for kindling,
burning wood for heat and food,
Hunting for food to cook.
Quiet, peaceful and calm,
nice people, everywhere you go
Sharing their food and
Sharing their ways of
the things they do around, and
the horses run free
and laugh with their little
people on their backs with
joy, while the trees sway .
The country is my place.

—Driscoll, Grade 6

Drip

Slowly onto cold hard ground
drip drop drip drop
over and over
again until the slow dripping
starts to stop
then just as it quickly started, it slowed
That's how life is;
It drip drops, it slows
down then slowly dries up just like a
River without flow

—Flynn, Grade 6

The Seasons

In the cold winter,
white snow blows outside,
dogs whimper,
not wanting to be confined inside.

In the bright spring,
buds appear on the trees,
beautiful birds begin singing,
whoosh, goes the breeze.

In the hot summer,
people go to the beach,
the world is full of color,
dogs run outside off leash.

In the lovely autumn,
bright colored leaves fall,
feel the air full of freedom,
hear the wild geese call.

—Freya, Grade 6.

Stories in my Heart

My heart is full of stories
About dragons and witches and things
Trudging through snowy flurries
Or destroying magic rings.

They pile up in my head
Come tumbling out of my mouth
I can't seem to write them down instead
So the times when I'm silent are as small as a mouse.

Oh, how I wish
I could write down my words!
Alas, they never get finished
So I'm left chattering like the birds.

—*Iris, Grade 6*

Memories

I stumbled through the grassy field,
yellow stalks bowed and murmured as I passed.
Somber expressions, they did wield,
As I sat and remembered when I was here last.

The spacious field held sorrowful echoes,
of those I've too soon lost.
Sober thoughts it bestows,
around, they have been tossed.

I can't help but think,
of the ways things have changed.
All seemed to wince and shrink,
and fall and rearrange.

I felt like a small bird,
whose wings have been taken.
Whose one sight has been blurred,
and all has been shaken.

Eventually I rose, and fell
but rose again to reach,
a story I sometimes need to tell,
to let go of the pain that came from each.

—*Iris, Grade 6*

I have to write a
Pretty poem with lots of
description although
I don't know what to
write; sometimes it's simple but
right now, it's quite hard
I sit here confused,
head in my hands, stumped and tired
Coming unwired
But not yet, because
I need to get a good grade
So I will find it
I think I have
Something going pretty well
Something in the air is different
Static, electric
Air tingles with energy
Excitement courses through me
My words dancing on
The page, swirling and spinning
Whimsical haiku

—Isa, Grade 6

Rain and Shine

Bolt of light as bright as the sun,
strike of sound that shakes the ground
a form of fire tumbling down.

Meanwhile, ocean waves crash on the shore
Seagulls sway and "keow" from above
Animals skipping in safety and security

Back in the storm, wild animals are fleeing
People not even stepping an inch on their porch
Everywhere drenched in fear and fright
Pets crouch in corners, quickly trying to hide from the storm

On the other side of the country,
People wade in the somewhat warm water
Not even noticing that in one place
a storm is shaking the ground and people are
rushing to a shelter or safety.
The hot beach is still and the tides getting larger
Everyone happy and carefree,
love and happiness in the air

The storm has ended, though the sky is still grumbling,
everyone safe and sound once again.

—Isabella, Grade 6

Crime Scene

Two people have gone mysteriously missing, something horribly wrong.
Herald the detective will solve the concealed crime,
Eric is one suspect; he runs a bar.
Ann is another, the beautiful wife of the magnificent mayor,
Nobody knows who it is.
Suspect Three says they saw Emily at the bar with Ann, her best friend;
Westin Suspect Three is the well dressed mayor.
Emily was with her great friend Ann and the sketchy guy, Bob.
Remember this, Bob and Emily are the missing people.
"I don't know who it is!" exclaimed Herald.
See the mess at the bar, beer everywhere!
And the cat is yelling fiercely at the glass that dared to touch him.
Nobody knows who did it.
Nobody but me, for the answer is in this poem.

—Isidor, Grade 6

Winter Begins

The wind quietly russells through the forest,
the squirrels scurried into the trees.
They were startled and stressed,
they feel a warm summer breeze,

Soon the forest will be its greenest,
buzzing on baby's breath with the bees.
The smell of pine and the sound of birds chirp chirp chirp,
the warmth of summer creates ease.

The flower so pretty yet so short lived,
By now the flowers must have bloomed.
The aroma of the flower so pretty and nice,
once winter begins the flowers are doomed,

The snow so cold, yet so bright.
The winter is so Freezing especially with the wind chill
Little flakes of ice dancing in the sky.
The winter has been fulfilled.

—Jacoby, Grade 6

Happiness of Summer

I dash through the grassy field
running to my house, though I have to yield.
Then I see a bug crawling on the ground
small and quiet, not making a sound.
It crawls up a stick and starts eating a leaf
then the bug crawled off in disbelief.
he stick seemed to sigh,
and then off the bug went, as it took to the sky.
Soon the little bug was out of my sight,
even as I tried to see it with all of my might.
Just that one little bug was a joy to my day,
and that's when I saw the pile of hay; I remembering what I was
      supposed to do:
Feed the chickens and the pigs too!
Summer is my favorite time of the year,
and that's how this season passed without a tear.

—Jade, Grade 6

The Smell of Seasons

The sweet smell of winter
Clear look of sharp icicles
The cold feel of snow

The sweet smell of summer
Illusionary heat waves
The wet feel of sweat

The sweet smell of fall
Windy look of tall trees in wind
The mild feeling breeze

The sweet smell of spring
Mud called to the kids to play
The cool feel of rain

—*Kasper, Grade 6*

Sunset, Sunrise

Beautiful sunset
 As pretty as a flower
Skies start to darken
Soon now the sunrise will sparkle upon us

The bright shining sky
 Birds *chirp chirping* the morning
Gazing, glaring sky
 Shining bright in my eyes

Glaring down on me
twisted colors sparkling down
Watching the sky fade
Sunset, Sunrise come again soon!

—Kinley, Grade 6

Lonely Oak Tree

The old tall oak tree sits in a vast green field, with nothing but the tree and grass for miles.
As the tree waits and waits, it hears a chirp in the distance, followed by a faint crying from a baby bird.
The crying suddenly stops as if the mom came back.
The oak tree had faith again, that there is something out there.

The tree hears faint walking behind it, it starts to get louder until it feels a gentle touch.
As the young boy feels the tree's rough bark, the tree asks, "Who are you?"
"I don't know anymore, I'm lost."
The tree stays quiet. "Why?"
The tree hears a thud from the boy collapsing onto the ground.

"What do you mean?" the boy replies.
" Are you all the way out here?"
Again the boy waits to respond: "I can't go back," the boy mutters.
The tree is shook by what he just said.
"What happened?" the tree asks, still in shock.
"They won't let me, I made a single mistake. that made my whole village hate me. So they made a decision to kick me out of my village."
The tree, taken aback from what he said, is quiet.
"I must go now, I have to find a place that wants me."
"If you must," the tree wept. "Visit me, I'm not moving."
 Tthe boy slightly chuckled, "I will."
The boy walked away, as he was far away he waved and cried "THANK YOU!"

The End?..

—Levi, Grade 6

Abc's

A is for **A**bandoned, like that night in the woods
B is for **B**ooks, like the one kept in my hood.
Cave is the **C**, the cave where I slept that cold night. **D**ark is the D, like the cave, the forest, that dark and fretful night.
E is for **E**arly, like the rising of the sun, **F**rigid is for F, like the mean bitter wind.
G is for **G**olden, like the sun that lit up the once dark woods.
H is the **H**awk that flies high above,
I is for **I**dle, for the squirrel in the tree,
J is the blue**j**ay, the one that chased the yellow bee.
K is the **K**ey, the one kept in my pocket.
L is the **L**ovely bright blue skies.
M is the **M**aggots, the ones crawling deep in the cave, **N**asty, like the creepy crawly bugs
O is the **O**wl resting up in the tree,
P is the majestic **P**ine with a hive of bees.
Q is for **Q**ueen snake, like the one basking on the rocks,
R is the **R**iver, rushing with excitement.
S is for **S**leeping, like I slept in the cave, that second dark night,
T is **T**he sun, that ends the dark scary fright of the night.
U if for **U**mbrella like I wish I had, that rainy glum morning.
V is for **V**ile, like the rotting deer in the woods,
W is for **W**hen, when can I go home?
X is the **X**antus murrelet, the one chirping up in the tree.
Y is for **Y**ears, how I lost track of how long I have been in these woods,
And Z is the **Z**ebra spider, crawling up the tree, going up oh so high.

—Louisa, Grade 6

An Apology

A is an apology I owe my sister for
B is a biology poster.
a job well done, a Crime, a test
that I'll Dare not confess.
Everything to see my sister Fail
Good thing I know How to disappear.
I know my crime thick and thin
I'll Jump away if it's mentioned.
sister Knowing I am guilty,
Losing control in the hole
I dug Myself deeper in.
Now was the time to surrender,
"O'brother" my sister said
I Pleaded for my soul
she Questioned me then
Right to the parents
She marched.
To the room I was headed
the Unison of stomps down hall shook me,
I must think Very quickly, I thought.
Then a light bulb Went off. out the window I'll jump
eXhausted I ran around the house.
whY I did this, I do not know
Maybe because she was adoZe.

—*Lowell, Grade 6*

A Midwinter's Night Dream

When you sneak outside to the wintery night
on a full December moon
the frosty cold will bite you
as soon as you unlatch the door.
You'll hold your toasty indoor breath
until you almost burst.
Then you'll let it out in a cloud of steam
that hovers and drifts away
as your lungs fill
with needle sharp air
that burns as it goes down your throat.
You'll blink in the shining moonlight
as you take in the sight
of the frosty moonlit night.
Windswept snow spreads in soft peaks
like a downy blanket over the world.
The white coated trees cast long dark shadows
that loom on the glowing white powder.
Their bare branches are skeletal fingers that reach longingly up to the sky
but you won't feel afraid
when you sneak out to the wintery night
on a full December moon.

—Marissa, Grade 6

Wild strawberries

Fresh wild strawberries
hang from the bush in summer
until autumn comes

Cozy colors come
Reds and yellows everywhere
The plants are dormant

Little hidden plants
under a blanket of snow
'till spring comes again

—Mason, Grade 6

Green Grass

Green as the grass
from the harsh past.

Green as strong leaves
on the green trees.

Green as the the eyes
of the smog skies.

Green is the shine
of the prime time.

Green as the soft grass
on the hard green ground.

The one that gets stomped on,
ripped up, and thrown around.

But green will recover
green will be okay.

Green we can count on
to save the day.

—Mila, Grade 6

Soccer

I shoot the round ball
so fiercely it flies
into the goal
it quickly falls

The defenders try
and the goalie dives
as they watch the ball quickly whiz by.

After that kick, it's shaped like a bean
it lands on the ground
Of gorgeous green grass
almost as if

it ran out of gas.

—Natalie, Grade 6

Sunset

Leafless lowering limbs,
High in crisp, brisk air.
Slowly bright light dims,
Down dips the sun so fair.

Like a glowing, astounding apocalypse,
Taking our world by surprise,
Beauty like an eclipse,
Happiness shall arise.

Deep red and bright yellow dance in the sky,
Hulking mountains silhouetted as the sun seems to splinter.
I spy with my little eye,
A beautiful sunset in winter.

—Ned, Grade 6

Winter

Flying down long runs
entering a world of dreams
Skiing is fun, cold

Light snow fell slowly
woods smiling, glittering white
Powder under skies

Observing snowflakes
the longer they stay out the
More they look like lakes

—Olivier, Grade 6

Coronavirus

The townspeople are weeping
the daily journal is stacking
the gossip is growing
as our people are lacking like a stop sign old and rusty.

And the curse on us is growing like a fungus
and the people are knowing
and we all need some sign.
Hey, they're joking.

I'm acting odd, jerking and gross.
I barely know my friends, they're engrossed;
I can not be close to anyone it seems,
So when will this end? Please tell me!

As I look away towards all I know
and I meet the blindness
of the dreaded virus
 Is it, it is . . . Coronavirus.

—Owen, Grade 6

A is for...

A is for **A**rms that welcome you in, with warmth and **B**eautiful love. Did you see what I did there? The **B** was already said. The **C** is for **C**aring and not wanting to flee like the birds migrating to the south. **D** is for dead, like the ones that you've lost, and now you feel dry in the mouth. **E** as in **E**verything that you've gone through, but you are **F**ierce and brave and calm. You are dreading the weight of the sand in your palm, but if you open up, and **G**ive it a **G**o, then maybe you'd love it; **Y**ou never know! **H**elp is what you give to the people you love. **I** for **I**ndigo, one of the prettiest flowers of all. It brings you **J**oy to look at. **K** is **K**ey, as in the one to your heart, which, of course is as sweet as a tasty tart. **L** is for **L**ove, **L**ovely, **L**iving, and **L**ife, the amazing things that make you feel right. **M M**eaning the **M**oon, kissing you goodnight. **N** is someone yelling "**N**o! Please don't go!" as you slowly walk away all **O**n your **O**wn. **P** is for **P**erfect, though there is no such thing as everything somebody wants or needs. **Q** is the **Q**uest you've been waiting for, such a crazy time, you drop to the floor. **R**est, now, for you have had a long day, but the memories you will keep in **S**tore. They love you a little more **T**han **t**o **t**he moon and back. They **U**nderstand what you are saying and what you mean. **V** is for **V**ictorious, like what they think of you and once you are done with your quest they will think everything of you. The **W**orld has made the path that you took on this journey. The world can see through you like an **X** - Ray, but it won't; They will look straight at your eyes. **Y**ou are a wonderful, loving person and for the **Z**illionth time, **A**, is for amazing, just like you.

—Sarah, Grade 6

That Little Blue House

That little blue house on top of the hill,
even just thinking about it gives me a thrill.
That little blue house on top of the hill once saw a kid take a big spill.
The kid started shrieking and screaming, holding her knee because it
    was bleeding.
That little blue house on top of the hill,
even just thinking about it gives me a thrill.
That little blue house on top of the hill,
there once was a girl who took a big spill, she started screaming, her
    mother came out to help her start healing.
That little blue house on top of the hill,
sometimes I think of it and remember it still.

—*Scarlett, Grade 6*

Seasons

Summer
Walking through a calm plain
In the burning warm sun
Listening to crickets in the brush
This is so mundane!

Autumn
"Crunch, Crunch, Crunch" the leaves go in my leaf pile
That arks like the rainbow in the sky
Finding the way out, courageous corn field
This a the fall lifestyle

Winter
Winter sports I'm ready; there's a sled I've been handed
At Hubbard Park with beautiful sledding hills
Hot chocolate smooth and warm
This is too cold and gloomy, without spring I'm stranded

Spring
Warm in the day cool in the night, always more fun than winter
Cold that holds your fun tighter than a glove
Almost summer break; school's coming to an end
About to make the cycle, This pattern makes the cycle better

— Silas, Grade 6

Grass, Clouds, Outside

Ever surviving
Undying, eternally
Pretty green lush, grass

Drifting silently
Cute, fluffy, lovely, and soft,
Without a fuss, clouds

Lush grass, fluffy clouds
Sprint with speed, chew without haste
Wasting time, outside

—Taylor, Grade 6

Tiny Friend

Watching her parade through the park
The birch, quite a good spot to claim
Watching her bound after a fleeing lark
An elegant beast, hard to tame

Barging through a gauntlet of leaves
Brown, or golden, what color should I say?
Her new friends, taking treats like thieves
No, golden brown like the color of hay

She curls up by the fire with delight
"To bed for all, and no delay"
Preparing for the short night
Unbearably drowsy from the long day

—Theo, Grade 6

Main Street Middle School, Montpelier:
Chrissy Keegan's Sixth Grade Class

The Animal in Me

There is an animal in me . . .
Climb run gets silly and has a big Family.
Nasal barking calls,
grunts, chatters and
squealing sounds.
Running "PATTER PATTER PATTER!" He ran. Get to his jungle family
Before dark,
over the Big brown tall Trees as lively as a tiger and as peaceful
As Apple Blossoms
Then he came across
A big shining yellow banana just waiting
For him. It was candy to his eyes.
a Wonderful filling
Treat for him and his
Family to munch on.
He ran home in excitement
"PATTER PATTER PATTER!"
Through the deep green jungle.
Swinging free,
The Monkey returned home
in his worm cozy tree,
The animal in me is a monkey
And a monkey I will be.

—*Analee, Grade 6*

There is a emperor penguin in me, can't you see.

It has a chin, a head and a throat but it is not a goat.

Emperor penguins live on ice, And they're the best they're so nice.

They huddle together the young and old, As they take turns against the cold.

Emperor penguins live on ice. The papa's the best, he's so nice.

I'm black and white, just look at me. We are Emperor penguins, black and white.

Short and wobbly, an interesting sight. So we'll waddle to the water and dive right in!

They never leave others behind, But as a group they never mind!

They are black and white, hard to see at night.

They run from seals but don't worry they don't steal.

—Andrew, Grade 6

There is an animal in me

I like to stay in the water and never get out of the water. If I did, I'd be dead.

It might seem tiny but I'm big with a school of friends.

I'm fancy and smooth because I have gold skin.

I'm friendly as a person.

I'm small but I'm a fast feeder.

My skin is gold and as smooth as a pubble.

I'm smart as a person.

I'm shy as wild things.

Do you Guess my animal? I'm a . . . Goldfish!

There is a goldfish in me in my soul,and my mind.

—Anisa, Grade 6

There is a otter in me
The otter is playful
Playing around with friends on the beach
The otter jumps and dives in to the sea
 The otters are free
 otters are so skibidi
Otter can be Curious
Trying new things
Sliding around on the ground
There are old ones and new ones
Good ones and bad ones Just like me
There is an otter in me

—Calan, Grade 6

There is a horse in me

I am as fast as a train.
I fly with the wind
There is a horse in me
I am strong like a lion
I am a fierce tiger
There is horse in me
A tall horse in me
A small horse in me
There is an horse in me
I care for people
As people care for me
There is a horse in me
An elegant horse in me
A beautiful horse in me
There is a horse in me

—Eliana, Grade 6

Bark, Bark, Bark!
There is a puppy in me
With fur as soft as a blanket, and intelligent eyes as deep and dark as the depths of the sea
I Can be calm, but energetic at the same time
As lively as a dolphin and always ready to play
Smart and eager for adventures but loyal to friends and family too
I Will jump into the water on a sunny day
Forgiving, friendly, social, and outgoing
Likes to nap, but loves to play
A forever friend and hard working helper
I will slay the day away
Filled with joy and happiness and no matter what happens, always up for a good time
There is a puppy in me
A trickster and a daring friend
It lives inside of me and makes me thoughtful and friendly
It keeps me happy and energetic
There is a puppy in me

—Eliza, Grade 6

The animal in me

There is an animal in me,
We have a big personality.
Trunk like and elephant,
Small like a pig.
They live in rainforests.
Their fur,
An artist's pallet.
Lacandon,
Is where they are from.
We are shy, and inoffensive.
We are also reclusive,
They are important recyclers of nutrients,
Helping the soil and landscape thrive.
I shall always strive,
That someday they are not en peligro.
That someday they are not endangered.
They are my favorite.
We are strong,
Capable of many things.
We will always begin.
And I make my case here.
In me is a tapir.

—Ellie, Grade 6

The Chicken in me

There is a chicken in me
We have a lot in common, can't you see?
Watchful, intelligent, and shy
Many things they are and can be
Their thick fluffy feathers mask their body, yet their heart shines
    through
They have no ears, yet they are kind enough to listen
They can't fly, yet they are brave enough to have wings
They are brave enough to try

Cold winter nights come by, wind howls mean names,
The flock is always there
Quiet
Quiet as can be
But never lonely for the flock is always there

Summer's claws snatch winter away
Heat eats away at comfort
The floor is a pigsty
The room is an inch
Yet Home it'll always be

I am a chicken
And a chicken is me
There is a chicken in me
We have a lot in common, can't you see?

—Esther, Grade 6

Animal in me

There is an animal in me,
With fur as soft as the freshly fallen snow,
outside my window,
As independent as a tiger, just like me!
It likes to keep its heart kind, just like me!
It enjoys the security and safety of its family, just like me!
It is happy to care for those around it, just like me!
It munches and crunches on eucalyptus leaves, not like me!
It likes to sleep for up to 18 hours a day, not like me!
It likes to attack when scared, not like me!
We both might seem gentle but we are strong when we need to be!
Did you guess my animal it's a... Koala!
Koalas rest in my mind, my heart, and my soul. We might share many
    Differences but we have more similarities.

—Farzyah, Grade 6

The Animal In Me

I have a fox in me
I am quiet like a mouse
But strong, like a elephant
I am little sly
But I do not lie
I love the snow
But also summer
Swift like the wind
Smart like a orca
I prowl for food
I pounce on meat as you hear a sharp squeak
But first I feed my family
I play in the snow
But only until I need to go back in my den
I love the forest, and I feel almost as if the trees speak to me
I am smart, and clever
You may hear a thud but that is me, jumping in the snow
I feel the cold snow on my face, my paws, my whole body
This is where I belong
The northeast, Vermont, warm summers, brisk winters, beautiful all year round.
This is where I belong
My home, beautiful vermont
There is a fox in me.

—Freya, Grade 6

The animal in me

There is a monkey in me.
So spunky just like monkey.
The monkey loves the trees swinging with breeze.
Monkey eat all of the banana in this jungle the savanna.
monkey has a tussle do to all the curfuzzle.
Monkey look at the monkey bros and they tell him like he dont know.
he tell bro's that he knows.
He loves the jungle but he always fumbles when it comes to trouble.
This chunky monkey is soft as sock.
Big like banna im so agile people might think I'm fragile.

—Harry, Grade 6

The raccoon in me

There is an Raccoon in me
With paws small and able
Always curious
Sticking out it's little tail to keep himself stable
Most people are furious when they hear the clang and bang as it tips over your garbage
Always listening for new things to learn
It has small nimble fingers like me
It crawls through the dark of night as smoothly as a dolphin cuts through the water
It's intelligence is far superior even to the smartest animals
It is playful and social like me.

—Hazen, Grade 6

The animal in me

1   I am a lioness
Fierce and tough
That's the animal in me
I am a lioness
5   Strong and gruff,
That's the animal in me
I am a lioness
My roar is as loud as 5 rocket launches,
That's the animal in me
10   I am a lioness
Sneaking, hunting
With raised haunches
That's the animal in me
I am a lioness
15   A stalker
A huntress
That's the animal in me
I am a lioness
I am not arrogant or vein
20   That's the animal in me
I am a lioness
I will forever remain
Queen of the jungle
I am a lioness.

—Helen, Grade 6

The Animal In Me

There is an animal in me.
With the stripes of a tiger,
As sly as a fox.
It cries like the wind,
As it runs through the hills.

Sits still,
A statue sculpted from stone.
But as the wind blows its fur of silk,
It flicks its tail in annoyance
At this disturbance.

As solitary as a stoat that hides deep underground.
But social like a sheep,
It finds comfort in its flock.
Braver than the whole sky,
Yet scared of unknown.

Unique in so many ways of our own,
We are all cats in some way or another.
Sacred of alone,
But afraid of each other.
There is a cat in me.

—Isabelle, Grade 6

"There is an animal in me"

My animal`is clever
My animal is smart
My animal is as fast as a car
My animal sees through eyes like amber
My animal has ears like raddars
If my animal had a score it would be a 4
My animal sings throughout the forest like an animal chorus
Ow, ow, owww howls the wolf
My animal hunts in a pack that is a fact
My animal is strong
My animals nose is never wrong
My animal is powerful
The way another animal knows to stay away you say?
Let's just say . . . my animal has its ways

—Kai, Grade 6

The Animal In Me

There is a black cat inside of me,
Deep down where no one can see.
With fur as black as coal,
And eyes as yellow as gold.
It runs around with its paws,
The ground beneath its claws.
It makes me calm and kind.
Having a cat inside of me,
Simply just makes me feel like me.
There is a black cat inside of me.

—Khloee, Grade 6

There is ferret in me

With legs made for dancing
And clumsy little arms
With an outstanding face
And likes the charmes
With lots of grace
That hates the hens
They like to chase in the dens
They live in a den
They like to be free
That is the animal in me.

—Kira, Grade 6

There is a seal in me.
As imaginative as a chimpanzee.
And as playful as a puppy.
Barks like a wolf.
Woof woof woof
Claws like razors.
whiskers drape down its chin.
I wish I could hold my breath
underwater
like an elephant seal.
It lives in my heart.
And makes me happy.

—Layla, Grade 6

The Animal in Me

Strong, graceful, brave
Kind, protective, determined
There is a panda in me

Rolling in the soft grass fields
Eyes sparkling, eyes like shimmering emeralds
Newly found dew droplets coat the greenery

Friendly and bold, a heart of gold
No hiding under the thick layer of fur
Saying hello to others who pass

Queen of this forest of green
The one who no one dares to challenge
Invisible crown sits tall on her head

The bamboo forest smells fresh, mmm
Large paws grasp longingly, only catching air
Reaching for the closest piece, mouth open

To eat
And eat
And eat

—Layla, Grade 6

The animal in me

The animal in me
Is a
Sea Otter
splishing, splashing, swimming around in the water
Clear as seaglass
Crisp as an apple
The animal in me is
As curious as a kitten
With a story that is unwritten
Carefree, often found with friends or family
The animal in me is
Diving into the water, looking for food
Soaking in the sunlight, enjoying the mood
And when the day ends, I lay down on my back floating in the water
Daydreaming about the endless possibilities in the sea
That is the animal in me

—Mai, Grade 6

Animal in me

Animal in me. I am a raccoon tired in the day but lively in the night
 and yet I love to fight and after a fight I love to have a bite the tose
    from the mose.
Digging thru trash but always in a dash always hungry but always tired
    and always admired i admire the raccoon
Wearing a mask of cuteness and they always have a task.
A raccoon is the Exact opposite of A baboon But me and the raccoon
    are quite similar
 Unlike me and my cousin He's exact opposite of me, Maybe he is a
    baboon
Baboon and the raccoon friends after all
Raccoon is Nature's trashcan but also Nature's doll
I wish I was a raccoon sneaky but funny loves To get in people's
    business
And yet I hate to do the dishes.So soapy so gross so stinky But moist.
So cute, so loving so tiny and so fuzzy yet so vicious inside It will
    scratch you in fear but yet Also for joy.chiter chiter the fuzzy little
    ball gose
They trick you with their cute little fuzzy paws then turn those little
    paws into weapons they will Attack you But then run away in fear i
    admire the raccoon

—Rory, Grade 6

The otter inside me!

There is an otter inside me,
It's fun and as bright as day,
It lives inside my heart,
And I smile when it plays,
It gives me lots of energy,
It likes to nap in sun rays,
This otter is happy,
They might just waddle away,
It always tells the truth,
When It opens a yummy clam,
And it tastes very salty,
Its squeak of satisfaction,
Sounds like the roar of a lamb,
It has feet like a flipper,
That I wear when I swim,
The otter always acts chipper,
They eat alot but they are still very slim,
This otter lives by the bay,
Oh, there is an otter inside me,
But I wonder on some days,
I think about my otter,
And if it wants to swim away.

—Winnie, Grade 6

Main Street Middle School, Montpelier:
Windy Kelley's Fifth Grade Class

Wake Up

The light screams
Alarm beeps
Someone yells
I sink into my bed

And then some one turns on the lights
And pulls off my covers
What a great start to the day

—Cora, Grade 5

Meatball Day

Today is the meatball day hopefully it is a good one
Last meatball day my dad choked so hard he turned purple
I look at the sauce it is as red as blood

Everything is on the table ready to eat
My dad takes a bite of a meatball the size of a elephant
My dad starts choking really loud

He quickly turners as purple as a grape
He manages to cough it up on the table
It looks like a giant hairball

—Felix, Grade 5

A piercing arrow strikes a white dove,
a scarlet pool swims in bitter innocence
as feathers drop in a bloody disaster
as a red river flows in pitch inky black
building with murder each second streaming of regret,
the doves flight stopped by who?
What will unfold?

—*Grace, Grade 5*

Unicorns

Unicorns are cute
They love to hop, jump, and play
We all need a uni!

—*Hailey, Grade 5*

The Hungry Hot Dog

The fresh hot dogs were so hot
you bite
And it Whispers
eat more

Commands

But he doesn't
he goes and sleeps
and when he wakes up
he sees a hot dog on him
and the hot dogs swim
now that dog is huge

And it's acid turned him into a big pile of dust and bones

He wakes up
it was a dream

he goes into the kitchen and makes two hot dogs
the hot dog Whispers 500 now!!
He listens to the command and he
 explodes

and now a dog is finally half one
 and it was not a dream

—Holden, Grade 5

Ellen Ochoa The Astronaut

When space called
Ellen followed
When science called
Ellen followed
She took risks
She followed her passion
And when it took her to the moon
Ellen followed

—Holden, Grade 5

Winter Night

I sit by my window, looking outside
A bit of moonlight, lights up the sky
The moon and its glow
Lights up the snow
It almost feels like morning

—*Josie, Grade 5*

Lying in My Bed

Lying in my bed
Watching.Waiting
Hoping you come
What if you don't?

In the middle of the night
Here in my bed
Thinking about what I didn't do
Trying to sleep with all my might

What I wish I could do
Is say to you
Why did you do it?
And why couldn't I?

—Jude, Grade 5

Tacos

I love tacos
They are
Delicious
Burritos, they're okay
Buuuuuuuuuuut
I like
Tacos
Moooooore

Tacos
They're good
For food fights
But they
Are tasty as well
So many
Toppings
To have

Now if
You are
Like me
And full heartedly
Agree
We could discuss
Toppings
You and me and Tacos!

—Levi, Grade 5

My Perfect Wintery Day

My perfect wintery day is 6 million feet of snow.

Looking out my window and seeing snow, I don't think that microbes could survive out there.

There is no electricity, it feels like it's snowing inside the house.

The snow is as fluffy as my cat Patches, as white as the school paper, and as heavy as a planet.

I pull open the door and I take a walk into the snow.

As I stroll along, It leaves a tunnel in the shape of my body.

I wandered for a long time and all I saw was snow.

I was very cold while tiptoeing through the snow. I'm surprised I didn't freeze my nose off.

Why am I so cold?

After I shuffled out of the snow, I found out that I'm in New Hampshire.

There's sun, beaches, and the pool is open.

I find out I'm wearing a bathing suit.

I hiked through all of that snow wearing it?

I went swimming for the rest of the day.

I then woke up from a dream and noticed I was wearing a bathing suit.

—Mary, Grade 5

Frog

Frog is jumping on a log
In a thick marshy hog
Frog croaks with all his might
As he leaps off into the night

—Mateo, Grade 5

Shin Godzilla

It looms over your house
And tramples it

Unleashing it's wrath
Upon everything

When the sky glows purple
Better run

Never looks straight
But It can always see you

Evolving and bleeding
While it throws himself onto the ground

It's dark past
Is full of shadow

An invincible
Beast

The ground shakes
When it is on land

Earth trembles in
Fear

It's
Coming

—Max, Grade 5

Skiing

You go out
In the
Cold
To
Ski!
It's fun to do
Out in the
Cold,
Turn, Skid,
SWOOSH!
Your skis move down
The mountain like
Socks on a slippery floor
You ski all day
You ski all night
When you go back
Home you hope to
Do it again
Tomorrow

—Miles, Grade 5

Sports

Sports
Awesome, exciting
Shooting, blocking, stealing, cool, energetic
Jumping, sprinting, assisting
Jogging, hustling
Basketball

—Miles, Grade 5

Twilight

I hold my Blanket like the sand holds my feet at the beach
I wonder where the snow starts
the moonlight sparkling like the water
birds levitating in the big blue
the glowing light guiding my way
hello to the new day

—Natalie, Grade 5

Cardinal

Tweet, tweet the cardinal chirps
Hopping from branch to branch
A snowflake lands softly on my nose
Cold like ice

I sigh, and get up to go inside
But just then I look up
Right as the cardinal hops then flies away
And I remember

I remember a time of sun
Of gurgling brooks and big, full, trees
Of flowers swaying
In the warm summer wind

A time of laughter
And then it was gone
But all too suddenly
Alas

—Penny, Grade 5

Blurt,Blurt,Blurt!

Everyone is blurting, like a flock of geese.
It has to stop, before I blow my top!

We have to stop blurting, we will have to calm down.
People won't talk, like a bunch of sloths.

—Quincy, Grade 5

Black Bears

Super scary
 really loud

Fish Eaters
 all kinds of bears

Black brown Cubs
 very vicious

They can have up to five cubs
 but they usually have two to three cubs

Bears hibernate in the winter
 they hibernate with their cubs

Their families are so cute
 you have to be careful when they're crossing

—Tyler, Grade 5

When the Night Hits

The darkness is a black cat
where luck is forgotten,
a woman has hair like a dead leaf,
the house on 17th street is haunted,
 an owl is on a tree of moonlight as a dog is sleeping like a tree.
when the moon hits the sun it is awakened,
 strong wind that has hit the kitchen window.
You will have a cozy night
when the night hits.
Everyone is sleeping.

—Zara, Grade 5

Main Street Middle School, Montpelier:
Wendy McGuiggan's Fifth Grade Class

My friend
dedicated to Colette

Trapped in a cage never let out
Trapped from my true self
But she reveals me
Im my true self when shes around
When shes gone I make no sound
She is my best friend

Shes there for me when im sad
Makes me laugh when im down
Shes there for me without doubt
Shes kind and thoughtful
Shes my best friend

—*Aquilla, age 11*

Siblings

Siblings
Mean, nice
Younger, older
Doesn't matter
They're there for you
You're there for them
You're best friends
FOREVER

Siblings
Laugh, cry
Play, sleep
It doesn't matter
You are like a moon
And there a sun
Your best friends
FOREVER

—Ariana, age 10

One Piece

One piece is the best
One piece is an anime
Wait until your older

—Beckett, age 10

A winter night

A frisk windy night
Underneath the moon-lit stars
The snow falling down
It feels unreal
But its all just a winter night

—Dylan, age 11

The Light

Beyond the earth,
Beyond the moon,
Beyond the sun,
Beyond the stars,
There is a light,
A beacon to lost souls,
Calling,"Come,Come"

—Eamon, age 11

Living

Living is a gift
Living is a curse
Once the decision is made it can't be reversed
Life can challenge and help you a lot
Just remember how you got here and all that you fought
Something will change in your life so don't run
It will all seem so simple when your all done

—Hendrix, age 11

Poptarts™ are Great!

Poptarts are great because they're like cupcakes
Poptarts are great because they are the sugariest thing
Poptarts are great because they are the happy sun
Poptarts are great because they make you go POP!
Poptarts are great because they let you act natural
So if you are craving a snack…
Eat a Poptart.

—*Jubal, age 11*

Friends

Friends are kind
Friends are helpful
Friends are funny
Friends are supportive
Friends are our everything
Friends are our favorite people
Friends are caring
Friends are cool
Friends are helpful
Friends are our savers
Friends are the snow and you are the ground
Friends are how we know
Friends help us know
Friends are what makes us know
Friends keep us levitating
Friends are the sun on our rainy days
Friends help to make a rainbow
Friends are our therapist
Friends make us upset
Friends make us happy
Friends make us sad
Friends make us peaceful
Friends are the best
Friends are our distant family and our friends are our everything

—*Julia, age 10*

Vermont

Vermont is maple sweetness

Vermont is shaggy old dogs,sitting by a fire

Vermont is sugar on snow

Vermont is   the woodlands beautifully glowing in the moonshine

Vermont is noah kahan

Vermont is fir trees heavy with the fresh fallen snow

Vermont is 100 year old bookshops

Vermont is the freshly fallen snow, untouched

Vermont is hiking with my family sisa and noah far ahead

Vermont is skiing

Vermont is 31 loomis st

Vermont is home

—Julien, age 11

Haiku about my cat

Sleeping on the couch
Purring softly on my lap
Brightening my day

—Liam, age 11

Love Is . . .

Love is friends.
Love is family.
Love is hugs.
Love is a warm drink.
Love is a smile.
Love is perseverance.

But . . .

Love can be heartbreak.
Love can be treachery.
Love can be trust broken.
Love can be an obsession.
Love can be rejection.
Love can be death.

That's why we have to
Hold on to love,
For if we let it go,
All is dark.

—Lucy, age 10

Marble human

Hopping, jumping through the snow
Watching the river and how it just flows.
Snout black as night, tail white as moonlight
But, just as normal and human in the daylight
Happy being black and white.

—Sybl, age 11

Cats

Meow meow im a cat
The superior life form
Give me food now you—

—Will, age 10

Darkness

Darkness is . . . a new start
Darkness is . . . the sun's sleep
Darkness is . . . the stars day
Darkness is . . . moon's shine
Darkness is . . . day's blanket

—Zephryn, Grade 5

Main Street Middle School, Montpelier:
Melissa Parker's Fifth Grade Class

The frog croaks so loud
The ground is soaked and muddy
The river is so runny

The cool autumn breeze
The leaves fall from the big tree
The colors are fun

—Adeline, Grade 5

Lion in the grass
Hiding and hunting for food
The lion goes home.

—Amjad, Grade 5

Sunset

While the sunsets, I see scribbles of colors shading in the late night sky.
While the sunsets, the bottoms of fluffy clouds glimmer with an orange light.
While the sunsets, I see the lake give off an eerie dim pink light.
While the sunsets, I see the old creaky wooden rocking chair sway back and forth on the porch in the fading light of day.
While the sunsets, I listen to the grasshoppers chirp in the fields of tall grass.

—Atticus, Grade 5

Capturing a Sunset

Capturing a sunset over the waves in the ocean is so pretty.
The way it shines over the ocean glimmering and shining.
The sun is bright orange.

—Ben, Grade 5

Raspberry

The delicate body
The fluffiness of the red, juicy fruit
Fill them with water like a cup
Individual parts struggle to stay together
RASPBERRY

—Casper, Grade 5

Trees blow in the wind,
Flowers growing in the spring
Birds fly to their nest

Pumpkins and brown leaves
Wispy clouds, falling red leaves
Fall is so much fun.

—Cora, Grade 5

The thunder crashing
Makes me shiver in the cold
Pouring down on me

—Davin, Grade 5

Fire

Burning and charring
Flames flickering and flaring
Bright and full of light

—Declan, Grade 5

Snow day

The snow captivating my eyes,
not able to look away.
a single snowflake falling on my head,
big white sky's so, so calming
taking my breath away.

—Elsa, Grade 5

Angel
truthful, beautiful
loving, healing, understanding
slaying, sleeping, torturing
lying, cursing, ki!!i*g
heartless, ugly
Devil

—Emma, Grade 5

Skiing

Down the mountain
I like to ski at night
it was too dark, I hit a tree
OH NO!

—George, Grade 5

Seasons

Winter:
Air as cold as ice,
Branches swaying in the wind.
Snow softens the ground.

Spring:
Plants bursting with joy,
Animals come back to life.
A breath of fresh air.

Summer:
The heat has no end,
And all life is plentiful.
But nothing can last.

Fall:
Leaves under my feet,
 Crunching in the crispy air.
 A rainbow of shades.

—Ira, Grade 5

THE SCISSORS CUT ME!
    BLOOD WAS GUSHING DOWN MY HAND . . .
I got a bandaid

—Luca, Grade 5

In my own world money means nothing.
In my own world everyone is treated equal.
In my own world the unalive are still with us.
In my own world people take risks.
In my own world a smile brightens someone's day.
In my own world home means a safe place.
In my own world the yelling is quiet.
In my own world I know people are different but the same.
In my own world I am protected
In my own world I am loved

—Marlowe, Grade 5

In The Woods

In the woods, there are chirping birds in the morning.
In the woods, there is a fox sneaking by.
In the woods, there are vines draping over branches.
In the woods, there is sunshine, pouring through the trees.
In the woods there are deer running away in the blink of an eye.
In the woods, there is silence, as loud as a scream.
In the woods, there are colorful mushrooms, beautiful, but deadly.
In the woods, there are leaves falling to the forest floor.
In the woods, there are countless adventures to be had.
In the woods, there is always something new.

—Phoebe, Grade 5

Blue fox, blue eyes
Sitting in the cold, cold night
Blue fox in the night

—Rory, Grade 5

The breeze in the wind zips through my hair as I watch birds glide out of their nest
don't be afraid little one
the wind outside doesn't matter, it's the wind in our hearts that counts.

—Ryan, Grade 5

Summer

Brilliant green grass
In the sun brightly shining
The wind calmly blows

—Sabra, Grade 5

Nothing,
barren, boring.
running, fighting, living.
shrill, endless,
Something.

—Saeed, Grade 5

The stillness slowly eats me,
It scares me.
I want to move, to run
but i can't.
I can think, yet cannot move
To die alone in this frozen twisted word of sadness.

—Sarah, Grade 5

My home
Only fun stuff
Never want to leave
Tennis courts
People are nice
Eat the best food
Love the bridges
I could stay forever
Even cousins like it here
Run a 5k

—Sebastian, Grade 5

Autumn evening

Trees blow in the wind
On a crisp autumn evening
Day breaks into night.

—Teo, Grade 5

Rumney School, Middlesex: Diana Costello's Fourth and Fifth Grade Class

Book Light

The small, blue book light
keeps the words so bright
even the sun itself is jealous.
Flick, Flick

—Angel, age 8

My Dog

My dog,
wild as a flooding river,
happy as a butterfly getting sweet nectar
white chest, black back
fast as a cheetah
hair as curly as mac and cheese
watching her run is so majestic!

—Blakely, age 9

The River

The river is greedy swallowing anything it can,
The river is calm, flowing gently down,
The river is mean with dangerous rapids
and wild waves that go whoosh
The river is funny,
it tickles my toes
like a feather.

—*Bodhi, age 8*

Markers

Blue, green markers
waiting for someone to pick them up
and make them dance,
Gliding on top of the white boards
Sometimes markers sound like shhhhh
or a weeeee sound,
They sway like Mexican dancers.

—*Djuna, age 8*

My Cousins Shoes

The laces are pink as pigs' noses
and purple striped
 like Alfaba's purple socks
They are laced
 like the stars above our heads
that come out at the end of a stunning sunset.
He wears them everywhere
They match his personality
 and his hair perfectly!

—*Edda, age 10*

Leaves

In early summer they're green and dainty,
like royalty, dressing the tree,
expecting the squirrels to bow down to them.
In mid autumn they gracefully dance down on the wind.
Twirling and twisting to the ground.
A rainbow of colors and more.
When they touch down they patiently wait
for another opportunity
to serve their goddess
the tree.

—*Elka, age 10*

Soccer

When you kick the ball
 it's like
 a falcon soaring through the sky
 right into the net like a bullet.

—Evan, age 10

Birds

I see birds soaring
 in the pink, dark sky
 like a feathery plane
sometimes all alone
birds cut the sky
day and night
with gold,silver,orange and red
 feathers falling like birds taking haircuts

—Fergus, age 8

Dweeb, my dog

Dweeb is as smart as a teacher
 and as lazy as a male lion
He has a little, black spot on his white head
It makes him look like a cow
He is the best thing that
ever happened to me.

—GG, age 8

Dragonfly

Zip! Zoom! rapid flashes
fly by like lightning.
Look at the green, black and purple go!
Finally, one lands by the lake
then it's still as a stake
taking a drink
it calms down
but in a blink
of an eye
it starts flying again
zooming by with its friends

—Lucciana, age 9

Fish Food

Fish food ~
pink, yellow and red dehydrated fish!
It silently hits the water
like leaves falling from the sky.
And fish speed to get it!

—Sam, age 8

My Black Lab

His name was Midnight
his short legs,
zooming to my sister's tree house
He snuggled with me when I was sick
We played tug of war
He was a very good dog

—Trinity, age 9

Union Elementary School, Montpelier:
Sarah Voorhis's Third Grade Class

School

I really like my school
I think it is really quite cool
I got friends [a bunch]
I really like lunch
But I am a fool in school

—Aria, age 9

A Limerick

Is the room hot or cold or not
It is definitely always gonna be hot
It's really sad
It's pretty bad
When the room is never not hot

—Asher, Grade 3

Fantastic
Remarkable
Awesome
Not nerdy
Cool
Efficient
Super

—*Frances, Grade 3*

A Limerick

There once was a creature who was a cat
And that cat wanted to catch a bat
But the bat decided to flee
So the cat climbed up a tree
The cat caught and ate the bat and got very fat

—*Freya, Grade 3*

Basketball

Basketball is fun
Amazing shots
Skilled moves
Kids shooting baskets
Endurance
Tall hoops
Boys passing
Always cool
Long shots
Let's do this

—Hunter, age 8

A Cinquain

Sister
Younger sibling
Playing singing dancing
Eleanor makes me feel happy
Sibling

—Josie, Grade 3

Soccer

Super fun
Optional game to play
Cool
Creative plays
Educational game
Referees stink

—Myles, Grade 3

Foxes

Soft and furry sprinting through the forest
Sleek and sneaky in the shadows
In the den nice and cozy
Sun rises in the morning
Time for breakfast
Found some berries

—Penny, age 8

Snakes

Some snakes have venom
No snakes have feet
All snakes have scales
Kind of creepy
Every snake has fangs
Snakeskin is cool

—Saskia, age 8

I like drawing little thingies
Some of them will sneeze
ah-AH CHOO!!!
Belong in zoo
Some in winter will freeze

—Tali, Grade 3

The Kellogg-Hubbard Library is a free, non-profit public library that serves the city of Montpelier and the towns of Berlin, Calais, East Montpelier, Middlesex, and Worcester; a population over 18,000. KHL has operated continuously as a library since 1895, only closing briefly for a polio epidemic in 1917, the Spanish Flu in 1918, the great flood of 1927, the flood of 1992, the Covid-19 pandemic of 2020, and the flood of 2023. Its mission is to empower community members to become lifelong learners by providing easy access to materials, online resources, programs, and a welcoming place.

www.ingramcontent.com/pod-product-compliance
Lightning Source LLC
Chambersburg PA
CBHW030441090526
44586CB00044B/458